CROCK·POT
◆ THE ORIGINAL SLOW COOKER ◆

COOKBOOK
&
RECIPE CARDS

Publications International, Ltd.

Material on pages 4, 5, 8, 12, 14, 18, 24, 26, 28, 30, 32, 36, 38, 40, 41, 42, 44, 48, 50, 52, 54, 56, 58, 59, 60, 62, 64, 66, 70, 72, 74, 78, 80, 82, 84, 88, 98 bottom, 100 bottom, 102 top, 104 top, 108, 110, 112 top, 114, 116, 118, 120 bottom, 122, 124, 126, 128, 130, 132 bottom, 134, 138, 140 and 142 bottom © Sunbeam Products, Inc. doing business as Jarden Consumer Solutions. All rights reserved. All other material and recipes © Publications International, Ltd.

CROCK-POT® and the **CROCK-POT®** logo are registered trademarks of Sunbeam Products, Inc. used under license.

Pictured on the front cover Pictured on the front cover *(from top left):* Maple-Glazed Meatballs *(page 6),* Herbed Fall Vegetables *(page 72),* Cannellini Minestrone Soup *(page 30)* and Barbecued Pulled Pork Sandwiches *(page 42).*

Pictured on the back cover: Chicken Tortilla Soup *(page 32).*

ISBN-13: 978-1-4127-4936-7
ISBN-10: 1-4127-4936-0

Library of Congress Control Number: 2008941395

Manufactured in China.

8 7 6 5 4 3 2 1

Preparation/Cooking Times: Preparation times are based on the approximate amount of time required to assemble the recipe before cooking, baking, chilling or serving. These times include preparation steps such as measuring, chopping and mixing. The fact that some preparations and cooking can be done simultaneously is taken into account. Preparation of optional ingredients and serving suggestions is not included.

contents

recipes to share

slow cooker
hints and tips

Slow Cooker Sizes

Smaller slow cookers, such as 1- to 3½-quart models, are the perfect size for singles, a couple, empty-nesters and also for serving dips.

While medium-size slow cookers (those holding somewhere between 3 quarts and 5 quarts) will easily cook enough food at a time to feed a small family, they are also convenient for holiday side dishes or appetizers.

Large slow cookers are great for large family dinners, holiday entertaining and potluck suppers. A 6- to 7-quart model is ideal if you like to make meals in advance and have dinner tonight and store leftovers for another day.

Types of Slow Cookers

Current models of **CROCK-POT®** slow cookers come equipped with many different features and benefits, from auto cook programs, to stovetop-safe stoneware to timed programming. Visit **www.crockpot. com** to find the slow cooker that best suits your needs and lifestyle.

Cooking, Stirring, and Food Safety

CROCK-POT® slow cookers are safe to leave unattended. The outer heating base may get hot as it cooks, but it should not pose a fire hazard. The heating element in the heating base functions at a low wattage and is safe for your countertops.

Your slow cooker should be filled about ½- to ¾-full for most recipes unless otherwise instructed. Lean meats such as chicken or pork tenderloin will cook faster than meats with more connective tissue and fat such as beef chuck or pork shoulder. Bone-in meats will take longer than boneless cuts. Typical slow cooker dishes take approximately 7 to 8 hours to reach the simmer point on LOW and about 3 to 4 hours on HIGH. Once the vegetables and meat start to simmer and braise, their flavors will fully blend and meat will become fall-off-the-bone tender.

According to the USDA, all bacteria are killed at a temperature of 165°F. It is important to follow the recommended cooking times and not to remove the lid often, especially early in the cooking process when heat is building up inside the unit. If you need to remove the lid to check on your food or are adding additional ingredients, remember to allow additional cooking time to ensure food is cooked through and tender. Large slow cookers, the 6- to 7-quart sizes, may benefit from a quick stir halfway during the cook time to help distribute heat and promote even cooking. It is usually unnecessary to stir at all as even ½ cup liquid will help to distribute heat, and the crockery is the perfect medium for holding food at an even temperature throughout the cooking process.

Oven-Safe

All **CROCK-POT®** slow cooker removable crockery inserts may (without their lids) be used in ovens at up to 400°F safely. Also, all **CROCK-POT®** slow cookers are microwavable without their lids. If you own another brand slow cooker, please refer to your owner's manual for specific crockery cooking-medium tolerances.

Frozen Food

Frozen food or partially frozen food can be successfully cooked in a slow cooker; however, it will require longer cooking than the same recipe made with fresh food. Using an instant-read thermometer is recommended to ensure meat is fully cooked.

Pasta and Rice

If you are converting a stovetop recipe to be made in a slow cooker and the recipe calls for uncooked pasta, cook it on the stovetop just until slightly tender before adding to slow cooker. If you are converting a recipe that calls for cooked rice, stir in raw rice with the other ingredients; add ¼ cup extra liquid per ¼ cup of raw rice.

Beans

Beans must be softened completely before combining with sugar and/or acidic foods. Sugar and acid have a hardening effect on beans and will prevent softening. Fully cooked canned beans may be used as a substitute for dried beans.

Vegetables

Root vegetables often cook more slowly than meat. Cut vegetables accordingly to cook at the same

rate as meat, large or small, or lean versus marbled, and place near the sides or bottom of the stoneware to facilitate cooking.

Herbs

Fresh herbs add flavor and color when added at the end of the cooking cycle, but for dishes with shorter cook times, hearty, fresh herbs such as rosemary and thyme hold up well. If added at the beginning, many fresh herbs' flavor will dissipate over long cook times. Ground and/or dried herbs and spices work well in slow cooking and may be added at beginning. The flavor power of all herbs and spices can vary greatly depending on their particular strength and shelf life. Use chili powders and garlic powder sparingly as these can sometimes intensify over the long cook times. Always taste the dish before serving and adjust seasonings, including salt and pepper.

Liquids

Excess liquid can be cooked down and concentrated after slow cooking on the stovetop or by removing the meat and vegetables from the **CROCK-POT®** slow cooker, stirring in cornstarch or tapioca and setting the slow cooker to HIGH. Cook on HIGH about 15 minutes or until juices are thickened.

Milk

Milk, cream, and sour cream break down during extended cooking. When possible, add them during last the 15 to 30 minutes of cooking, until just heated through.

Fish

Fish is delicate and should be stirred in gently during the last 15 to 30 minutes of cooking time. Cook until just cooked through and serve immediately.

appetizers and snacks

Maple-Glazed Meatballs

Cook Time: 5 to 6 hours (LOW)

1½ **cups ketchup**

1 **cup maple syrup or maple-flavored syrup**

⅓ **cup reduced-sodium soy sauce**

1 **tablespoon quick-cooking tapioca**

1½ **teaspoons ground allspice**

1 **teaspoon dry mustard**

2 **packages (about 16 ounces each) frozen fully cooked meatballs, partially thawed and separated**

1 **can (20 ounces) pineapple chunks in juice, drained**

1. Combine ketchup, maple syrup, soy sauce, tapioca, allspice and mustard in 4½-quart **CROCK-POT®** slow cooker.

2. Carefully stir meatballs and pineapple chunks into ketchup mixture.

3. Cover; cook on LOW 5 to 6 hours. Stir before serving. Serve warm; insert cocktail picks, if desired.

Makes about 48 meatballs

Tip: For a quick main dish, serve meatballs over hot cooked rice.

Warm Blue Crab Bruschetta

Cook Time: 3 hours (LOW)

4 cups peeled, seeded and diced Roma or plum tomatoes

1 cup diced white onion

2 teaspoons minced garlic

⅓ cup olive oil

2 tablespoons balsamic vinegar

½ teaspoon dried oregano

2 tablespoons sugar

1 pound lump blue crabmeat, picked over for shells

1½ teaspoons kosher salt

½ teaspoon cracked black pepper

⅓ cup minced fresh basil

2 baguettes, sliced and toasted

1. Combine tomatoes, onion, garlic, oil, vinegar, oregano and sugar in 4½-quart **CROCK-POT®** slow cooker. Cover; cook on LOW 2 hours.

2. Add crabmeat, salt and pepper. Stir gently to mix, taking care not to break up crabmeat lumps. Cook on LOW 1 hour.

3. Fold in basil. Serve on toasted baguette slices.

Makes 16 servings

Serving Suggestion: Crab topping can also be served on Melba toast or whole-grain crackers.

Sausage and Swiss Chard Stuffed Mushrooms

Cook Time: 3 hours (HIGH)

2 **packages (6 ounces each) large mushrooms,* wiped clean**

4 **tablespoons extra-virgin olive oil, divided**

½ **pound bulk pork sausage**

½ **onion, finely chopped**

2 **cups chopped Swiss chard, rinsed**

¼ **teaspoon dried thyme**

2 **tablespoons garlic-and-herb-flavored dried bread crumbs**

1½ **cups chicken broth, divided**

Salt and black pepper

2 **tablespoons grated Parmesan cheese**

2 **tablespoons chopped fresh parsley**

*Use "baby bellas" or cremini mushrooms. Do not substitute white button mushrooms.

1. Coat inside of 5- to 6-quart **CROCK-POT®** slow cooker with nonstick cooking spray. Remove stems from mushrooms and hollow out caps. Brush inside and out using 3 tablespoons oil.

2. Heat remaining 1 tablespoon oil in medium skillet over medium heat. Crumble sausage into skillet and cook until browned. Transfer to medium bowl with slotted spoon.

3. Return skillet to heat. Add onion and cook until translucent. Stir in chard and thyme and cook just until chard wilts. Remove from heat. Stir in cooked sausage, bread crumbs and 1 tablespoon broth. Season with salt and pepper. Divide evenly among mushroom caps.

4. Pour remaining broth into **CROCK-POT®** slow cooker. Arrange mushrooms in broth. Cover; cook on HIGH 3 hours or until tender. Sprinkle with cheese and parsley before serving.

Makes 6 to 8 servings

Variation: If desired, place a small square of sliced Swiss cheese on each mushroom and continue cooking 15 minutes longer or until cheese is melted. Proceed as directed.

Honey-Glazed Chicken Wings

Cook Time: 6 to 8 hours (LOW) or 3 to 4 hours (HIGH)

3 **tablespoons vegetable oil, divided**

3 **pounds chicken wings, tips removed**

1 **cup honey**

½ **cup soy sauce**

1 **clove garlic, minced**

2 **tablespoons tomato paste**

2 **teaspoons water**

1 **teaspoon sugar**

1 **teaspoon black pepper**

1. Heat 1½ tablespoons oil in skillet over medium heat until hot. Brown chicken wings on each side in batches to prevent crowding. Turn each piece as it browns, about 1 to 2 minutes per side. Transfer with slotted spoon to **CROCK-POT®** slow cooker.

2. Combine honey, soy sauce, remaining 1½ tablespoons vegetable oil, and garlic in medium bowl. Whisk in tomato paste, water, sugar and pepper. Pour sauce over chicken. Cover; cook on LOW 6 to 8 hours or on HIGH 3 to 4 hours.

Makes 6 to 8 servings

Refried Bean Dip with Blue Tortilla Chips

Cook Time: 2 to 4 hours (LOW)

3 cans (16 ounces each) refried beans

1 cup prepared taco sauce

½ teaspoon salt

½ teaspoon black pepper

3 cups shredded Cheddar cheese, divided

¾ cup chopped green onions

2 packages (12 ounces each) blue tortilla chips

Combine refried beans, taco sauce, salt and pepper in large bowl. Spread one-third of bean mixture on bottom of 4½-quart **CROCK-POT®** slow cooker. Sprinkle evenly with ¾ cup cheese. Repeat layers, finishing with cheese layer. Sprinkle green onions evenly on cheese. Cover; cook on LOW 2 to 4 hours. Serve with blue tortilla chips for dipping.

Makes 10 servings

Creamy Artichoke-Parmesan Dip

Cook Time: 4 to 5 hours (LOW) or 2 to 2½ hours (HIGH)

- **2 cans (14 ounces each) artichoke hearts, drained and chopped**
- **2 cups (8 ounces) shredded mozzarella cheese**
- **1½ cups grated Parmesan cheese**
- **1½ cups mayonnaise**
- **½ cup finely chopped onion**
- **½ teaspoon dried oregano**
- **¼ teaspoon garlic powder**
- **4 pita breads, cut into wedges**
- **Assorted cut-up vegetables**

Place artichokes, mozzarella cheese, Parmesan cheese, mayonnaise, onion, oregano and garlic powder in 1½-quart or other small-sized **CROCK-POT®** slow cooker; mix well. Cover; cook on LOW 2 hours. Arrange pita bread wedges and vegetables on platter; serve with warm dip.

Makes 16 servings (about 4 cups)

Tip: When adapting conventionally prepared recipes for your **CROCK-POT®** slow cooker, revise the amount of herbs and spices you use. For example, whole herbs and spices increase in flavor while ground spices tend to lose flavor during slow cooking. You can adjust the seasonings or add fresh herbs and spices just before serving the dish.

Cereal Snack Mix

Cook Time: 3 to 4 hours (LOW) or 45 minutes (HIGH)

6 **tablespoons unsalted butter, melted**

2 **tablespoons curry powder**

2 **tablespoons reduced-sodium soy sauce**

1 **tablespoon sugar**

1 **tablespoon paprika**

2 **teaspoons ground cumin**

½ **teaspoon salt**

5 **cups rice squares cereal**

5 **cups corn squares cereal**

1 **cup tiny pretzels**

⅓ **cup lightly salted peanuts**

1. Pour butter in 4½-quart **CROCK-POT®** slow cooker. Stir in curry, soy sauce, sugar, paprika, cumin and salt. Stir in cereal, pretzels and peanuts. Cook, uncovered, on HIGH 45 minutes, stirring often to avoid sugar scorching.

2. Reduce **CROCK-POT®** slow cooker to LOW and cook, uncovered, 3 to 4 hours longer, stirring often. Let cool and transfer to large serving bowl.

Makes 20 servings

Chili Con Queso

Cook Time: 2½ to 3 hours (LOW)

1   **package (16 ounces) pasteurized processed cheese spread, cubed**

1   **can (10 ounces) diced tomatoes with green chiles**

1   **cup sliced green onions**

2   **teaspoons ground coriander**

2   **teaspoons ground cumin**

¾   **teaspoon hot pepper sauce**

Green onion strips (optional)

Hot pepper slices (optional)

Tortilla chips

1. Combine cheese spread, tomatoes, green onions, coriander and cumin in **CROCK-POT®** slow cooker; stir until well blended.

2. Cover; cook on LOW 2 to 3 hours or until hot.*

3. Garnish with green onion strips and hot pepper slices, if desired. Serve with tortilla chips.

Dip will be very hot; use caution when serving.

Makes 3 cups

Serving Suggestion: Serve Chili con Queso with tortilla chips. For something different, cut pita bread into triangles and toast them in a preheated 400°F oven for 5 minutes or until they are crisp.

Barbecued Meatballs

Cook Time: 4 hours (LOW)

2 **pounds (32 ounces) 95% lean ground beef**

1⅓ **cups ketchup, divided**

3 **tablespoons seasoned dry bread crumbs**

1 **egg, lightly beaten**

2 **tablespoons dried onion flakes**

¾ **teaspoon garlic salt**

½ **teaspoon black pepper**

1 **cup packed light brown sugar**

1 **can (6 ounces) tomato paste**

¼ **cup reduced-sodium soy sauce**

¼ **cup cider vinegar**

1½ **teaspoons hot pepper sauce**

Sliced green bell peppers (optional)

1. Preheat oven to 350°F. Combine ground beef, ⅓ cup ketchup, bread crumbs, egg, onion flakes, garlic salt and black pepper in medium bowl. Mix lightly but thoroughly; shape into 1-inch meatballs.

2. Place meatballs in 2 (15×10-inch) jelly-roll pans or shallow roasting pans. Bake 18 minutes or until browned. Transfer to 4½-quart **CROCK-POT®** slow cooker.

3. Mix remaining 1 cup ketchup, sugar, tomato paste, soy sauce, vinegar and hot pepper sauce in medium bowl. Pour over meatballs. Cover; cook on LOW 4 hours. Add jalapeño slices to mixture, if desired. Serve with cocktail picks.

Makes about 4 dozen meatballs

Barbecued Franks: Arrange 2 (12-ounce) packages or 3 (8-ounce) packages cocktail franks in slow cooker. Combine 1 cup ketchup with brown sugar, tomato paste, soy sauce, vinegar and hot pepper sauce in medium bowl; pour over franks. Cook according to directions for Barbecued Meatballs.

Sweet and Spicy Sausage Rounds

Cook Time: 3 hours (HIGH)

1 **pound kielbasa sausage, cut into ¼-inch-thick rounds**
⅔ **cup blackberry jam**
⅓ **cup steak sauce**
1 **tablespoon prepared yellow mustard**
½ **teaspoon ground allspice**

1. Place all ingredients in **CROCK-POT®** slow cooker; toss to coat completely. Cook on HIGH 3 hours or until richly glazed.

2. Serve with decorative cocktail picks.

Makes 3 cups

Soups
and stews

Roasted Corn and Red Pepper Chowder

Cook Time: 7 to 9 hours (LOW) or 4 to 5 hours (HIGH)

2   **tablespoons extra-virgin olive oil**

2   **cups fresh corn kernels or frozen corn, thawed**

1   **red bell pepper, cored, seeded and diced**

2   **green onions, sliced**

4   **cups chicken broth**

2   **baking potatoes, peeled and diced**

1   **teaspoon salt**

½   **teaspoon black pepper**

1   **can (13 ounces) evaporated milk**

2   **tablespoons minced flat-leaf parsley**

1. Heat oil in skillet over medium heat until hot. Add corn, bell pepper and green onions. Cook and stir until vegetables are tender and lightly browned, about 7 to 8 minutes. Transfer to **CROCK-POT®** slow cooker.

2. Add broth, potatoes, salt and pepper. Stir well to combine. Cover; cook on LOW 7 to 9 hours or on HIGH 4 to 5 hours.

3. Thirty minutes before serving, add evaporated milk. Stir well to combine and continue cooking. To serve, garnish with parsley.

Makes 4 servings

Northwest Beef and Vegetable Soup

Cook Time: 2 hours (HIGH), plus 4 to 6 hours (LOW)

2 tablespoons olive oil

1 pound lean stew beef, fat removed and cut into 1-inch cubes

1 medium onion, chopped

1 clove garlic, minced

3½ cups canned crushed tomatoes, undrained

1 can (15 ounces) white beans, drained and rinsed

1 buttercup squash, peeled and diced

1 turnip, peeled and diced

1 large potato, peeled and diced

2 stalks celery, sliced

2 tablespoons minced fresh basil

1½ teaspoons salt

1 teaspoon black pepper

8 cups water

1. Heat oil in skillet over medium heat until hot. Sear beef on all sides, turning as it browns. Add onion and garlic during last few minutes of searing. Transfer to 4½-quart **CROCK-POT®** slow cooker.

2. Add remaining ingredients. Gently stir well to combine. Cover; cook on HIGH 2 hours. Turn **CROCK-POT®** slow cooker to LOW. Cook on LOW 4 to 6 hours longer, stirring occasionally and adjusting seasonings to taste.

Makes 6 to 8 servings

Mushroom Barley Stew

Cook Time: 5½ hours (LOW) or 3 to 4 hours (HIGH)

1 **cup dried mushrooms**

1 **cup pearl barley, rinsed and sorted (about ½ pound)**

1 **package (10 ounces) fresh mushrooms, rinsed and thinly sliced**

2 **carrots, peeled and cut into ¼-inch dice**

2 **celery stalks, cut into ¼-inch dice**

1 **yellow onion, cut into ¼-inch dice**

1 **tablespoon fresh thyme**

2 **bay leaves**

1 **tablespoon tomato paste**

Salt and black pepper, to taste

8 **to 10 cups chicken or mushroom stock**

2 **tablespoons minced fresh parsley**

1. Place dried mushrooms in small bowl and cover with warm water. Set aside to soak 15 minutes or until softened. Transfer mushrooms and soaking liquid (taking care to discard any grit) to 4½-quart **CROCK-POT®** slow cooker.

2. Add barley, fresh mushrooms, carrots, celery, onion, thyme, bay leaves, tomato paste, salt and black pepper. Stir to combine then pour in stock.

2. Cover; cook on LOW 5½ hours or on HIGH 3 to 4 hours, or until barley and vegetables are tender. Add additional salt and pepper to taste before serving garnished with parsley.

Makes 8 to 10 servings

Cannellini Minestrone Soup

Cook Time: 6 to 8 hours (LOW) or 4 to 6 hours (HIGH)

4 cups chicken broth

1 can (14½ ounces) diced tomatoes, undrained

1 can (12 ounces) tomato-vegetable juice

2 cups escarole, cut into ribbons

1 cup chopped green onions

1 cup chopped carrots

1 cup chopped celery

1 cup chopped potatoes

¼ cup dried cannellini beans, sorted and rinsed

2 tablespoons chopped fresh chives

1 tablespoon chopped fresh flat-leaf parsley

¼ teaspoon salt

¼ teaspoon black pepper

2 ounces uncooked ditalini pasta

1. Place all ingredients except pasta, in 5-quart **CROCK-POT**® slow cooker. Stir well to combine. Cover; cook on LOW 6 to 8 hours or on HIGH 4 to 6 hours.

2. Add ditalini and stir again. Cover; cook 20 minutes before serving.

Makes 6 servings

Chicken Tortilla Soup

Cook Time: 6 hours (LOW) or 3 hours (HIGH)

4 **boneless skinless chicken thighs**

2 **cans (15 ounces each) diced tomatoes, undrained**

1 **can (4 ounces) chopped mild green chilies, drained**

½ **to 1 cup chicken broth**

1 **yellow onion, diced**

2 **cloves of garlic, minced**

1 **teaspoon ground cumin**

Salt and black pepper, to taste

4 **corn tortillas, sliced into ¼-inch strips and baked until crisp**

2 **tablespoons chopped fresh cilantro**

½ **cup shredded Monterey Jack cheese**

1 **avocado, peeled, diced and tossed with lime juice to prevent browning**

Lime wedges

1. Place chicken in 4½-quart **CROCK-POT®** slow cooker. Combine tomatoes with juice, chilies, ½ cup broth, onion, garlic and cumin in small bowl. Pour mixture over chicken.

2. Cover; cook on LOW 6 hours or on HIGH 3 hours, or until chicken is tender. Remove chicken from **CROCK-POT®** slow cooker. Shred with 2 forks. Return to cooking liquid. Adjust seasonings, adding salt and pepper and more broth, if necessary.

3. Just before serving, add tortillas and cilantro to **CROCK-POT®** slow cooker. Stir to blend. Serve in soup bowls, topping each serving with cheese, avocado and a squeeze of lime juice.

Makes 4 to 6 servings

Best Ever Chili

Cook Time: 10 to 12 hours (LOW)

1½ **pounds ground beef**

1 **cup chopped onion**

2 **cans (about 15 ounces each) kidney beans, drained, canning liquid reserved**

1½ **pounds plum tomatoes, diced**

1 **can (15 ounces) tomato paste**

3 **to 6 tablespoons chili powder**

1. Cook and stir beef and onion in large skillet over medium-high heat, stirring to break up meat, 10 minutes or until meat is no longer pink. Drain; transfer beef mixture to slow cooker.

2. Add kidney beans, tomatoes, tomato paste, 1 cup reserved bean canning liquid and chili powder to 4½-quart **CROCK-POT®** slow cooker; mix well. Cover; cook on LOW 10 to 12 hours or until tomatoes have softened completely.

Makes 8 serving:

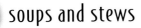

Chipotle Chicken Stew

Cook Time: 7 to 8 hours (LOW) or 3½ to 4 hours (HIGH)

1 **pound boneless skinless chicken thighs, cut into cubes**

1 **can (15 ounces) navy beans, rinsed and drained**

1 **can (15 ounces) black beans, rinsed and drained**

1 **can (14½ ounces) crushed tomatoes, undrained**

1½ **cups chicken broth**

½ **cup orange juice**

1 **medium onion, diced**

1 **chipotle pepper in adobo sauce, minced**

1 **teaspoon salt**

1 **teaspoon ground cumin**

1 **bay leaf**

Cilantro sprigs (optional)

1. Combine chicken, beans, tomatoes with juice, broth, orange juice, onion, chipotle pepper, salt, cumin and bay leaf in 4½-quart **CROCK-POT®** slow cooker.

2. Cover; cook on LOW 7 to 8 hours or on HIGH 3½ to 4 hours. Remove bay leaf before serving. Garnish with cilantro sprigs, if desired.

Makes 6 servings

Manhattan Clam Chowder

Cook Time: 6 to 8 hours (LOW) or 4 to 6 hours (HIGH)

3 **slices bacon, diced**

2 **stalks celery, chopped**

3 **onions, chopped**

2 **cups water**

1 **can (15 ounces) stewed tomatoes, undrained and chopped**

4 **small red potatoes, diced**

2 **carrots, diced**

½ **teaspoon dried thyme**

½ **teaspoon black pepper**

½ **teaspoon Louisiana-style hot sauce**

1 **pound minced clams***

*If fresh clams are unavailable, use canned clams; 6 (6½-ounce) cans yield about 1 pound of clam meat; drain and discard liquid.

1. Cook and stir bacon in medium saucepan until bacon is crisp. Remove bacon and place in **CROCK-POT®** slow cooker.

2. Add celery and onions to skillet. Cook and stir until tender. Place in **CROCK-POT®** slow cooker.

3. Mix in water, tomatoes with juice, potatoes, carrots, thyme, pepper and hot sauce. Cover; cook on LOW 6 to 8 hours or HIGH 4 to 6 hours. Add clams during last half hour of cooking.

Makes 4 servings

Tip: Shellfish and mollusks are delicate and should be added to the **CROCK-POT®** slow cooker during the last 15 to 30 minutes of the cooking time if you're using the high heat setting, and during the last 30 to 45 minutes if you're using the low setting. This type of seafood overcooks easily, becoming tough and rubbery, so watch your cooking times, and cook only long enough for foods to be done.

Easy Beef Stew

Cook Time: 8 to 12 hours (LOW)

2 **pounds beef for stew, cut into 1-inch cubes**

1 **can (4 ounces) mushrooms**

1 **envelope (1 ounce) dry onion soup mix**

⅓ **cup red or white wine**

1 **can (10 ounces) cream of mushroom soup, undiluted**

Hot cooked noodles

Combine all ingredients, except noodles, in **CROCK-POT®** slow cooker. Cover; cook on LOW 8 to 12 hours. Serve over noodles.

Makes 4 to 6 servings

Tip: Browning the beef before cooking it in the **CROCK-POT®** slow cooker isn't necessary but helps to enhance the flavor and appearance of the stew. If you have the time, use nonstick cooking spray and brown the meat in a large skillet before placing it in the **CROCK-POT®** slow cooker; follow the recipe as written.

Savory Chicken and Oregano Chili

Cook Time: 8 to 10 hours (LOW) or 4 to 5 hours (HIGH)

3 **cans (15 ounces each) Great Northern or cannellini beans, drained**

3½ **cups chicken broth**

2 **cups chopped cooked chicken**

2 **medium red bell peppers, cored, seeded and chopped**

1 **medium onion, peeled and chopped**

1 **can (4 ounces) diced green chiles**

3 **cloves garlic, minced**

2 **teaspoons ground cumin**

1 **teaspoon salt**

1 **tablespoon minced fresh oregano**

1. Place beans, broth, chicken, bell peppers, onion, chiles, garlic, cumin and salt in 5- to 6-quart **CROCK-POT®** slow cooker. Mix well to combine. Cover; cook on LOW 8 to 10 hours or on HIGH 4 to 5 hours.

2. Stir in oregano before serving.

Makes 8 servings

main dishes

Barbecued Pulled Pork Sandwiches

Cook Time: 10 to 12 hours (LOW) or 5 to 6 hours (HIGH)

1 (2½ pounds) pork shoulder roast

1 bottle (14 ounces) barbecue sauce

1 tablespoon fresh lemon juice

1 teaspoon brown sugar

1 medium onion, chopped

8 hamburger buns or hard rolls

1. Place the pork roast in 4½-quart **CROCK-POT®** slow cooker. Cover; cook on LOW for 10 to 12 hours or on HIGH for 5 to 6 hours.

2. Remove the pork roast from the stoneware. Shred the pork with 2 forks. Discard any liquid in the stoneware. Return the pork to the stoneware; add the barbecue sauce, lemon juice, brown sugar and onion. Cook on HIGH for 1 hour or on LOW for 2 hours.

3. Serve the pork on hamburger buns or hard rolls.

Makes 8 servings

Note: This kid-popular dish is sweet and savory, and most importantly, extremely easy to make. Serve with crunchy coleslaw on the side.

Tip: For a 5, 6 or 7-quart **CROCK-POT®** slow cooker, double all ingredients, except for the barbecue sauce. Increase the barbecue sauce to 21 ounces.

Stuffed Chicken Breasts

Cook Time: 5½ to 6 hours (LOW) or 4 hours (HIGH)

6 **boneless skinless chicken breasts**

8 **ounces feta cheese, crumbled**

3 **cups chopped fresh spinach leaves**

⅓ **cup oil-packed sun-dried tomatoes, drained and chopped**

1 **teaspoon minced lemon peel**

1 **teaspoon dried basil, oregano or mint**

½ **teaspoon garlic powder**

Freshly ground black pepper, to taste

1 **can (15 ounces) diced tomatoes, undrained**

½ **cup oil-cured olives***

Hot cooked polenta

If using pitted olives, add to CROCK-POT® slow cooker in the final hour of cooking.

1. Place chicken breast between 2 pieces of plastic wrap. Using tenderizer mallet or back of skillet, pound breast until about ¼ inch thick. Repeat with remaining chicken.

2. Combine feta, spinach, sun-dried tomatoes, lemon peel, basil, garlic powder and pepper in medium bowl.

3. Lay pounded chicken, smooth-side down, on work surface. Place about 2 tablespoons feta mixture on wide end of breast. Roll tightly. Repeat with remaining chicken.

4. Place rolled chicken, seam-side down, in 4½-quart **CROCK-POT®** slow cooker. Top with diced tomatoes with juice and olives. Cover; cook on LOW 5½ to 6 hours or on HIGH 4 hours. Serve with polenta.

Makes 6 servings

Tex-Mex Beef Wraps

Cook Time: 8 to 9 hours (LOW) or 3½ to 4½ hours (HIGH)

1 **tablespoon chili powder**

2 **teaspoons ground cumin**

1 **teaspoon salt**

¼ **teaspoon ground red pepper**

1 **boneless beef chuck pot roast (2½ to 3 pounds), cut into 4 pieces**

1 **medium onion, chopped**

3 **cloves garlic, minced**

1 **cup salsa, divided**

12 **(6- to 7-inch) flour or corn tortillas, warmed**

1 **cup shredded Cheddar or Monterey Jack cheese**

1 **cup chopped tomato**

¼ **cup chopped cilantro**

1 **ripe avocado, diced**

1. Blend chili powder, cumin, salt and red pepper. Rub meat all over with spice mixture. Place onion and garlic in bottom of 4½-quart **CROCK-POT®** slow cooker; top with meat. Spoon ½ cup salsa over meat. Cover and cook on LOW 8 to 9 hours, or on HIGH 3½ to 4½ hours.

2. Remove meat from **CROCK-POT®** slow cooker; place on plate and use 2 forks to shred meat. Skim off and discard fat from cooking liquid; return meat to juices and mix well. Adjust seasonings. Place meat on warm tortillas; top with cheese, tomato, cilantro and avocado. Roll up to enclose filling. Serve with remaining salsa.

Makes 6 servings

Scallops in Fresh Tomato and Herb Sauce

Cook Time: 6 to 8 hours (LOW) and 15 minutes (HIGH)

2   **tablespoons vegetable oil**

1   **medium red onion, peeled and diced**

1   **clove garlic, minced**

3½ **cups fresh tomatoes, peeled***

1   **can (12 ounces) tomato pureé**

1   **can (6 ounces) tomato paste**

¼   **cup dry red wine**

2   **tablespoons chopped flat-leaf parsley**

1   **tablespoon chopped fresh oregano**

¼   **teaspoon black pepper**

1½ **pounds fresh scallops, cleaned and drained**

*To peel tomatoes, place one at a time in simmering water about 10 seconds. (Add 30 seconds if tomatoes are not fully ripened.) Immediately plunge into a bowl of cold water for another 10 seconds. Peel skin with a knife.

1. Heat oil in skillet over medium heat until hot. Add onion and garlic. Cook and stir 7 to 8 minutes, or until onions are soft and translucent. Transfer to 4½-quart **CROCK-POT®** slow cooker.

2. Add tomatoes, tomato purée, tomato paste, wine, parsley, oregano and pepper. Cover; cook on LOW 6 to 8 hours.

3. Turn **CROCK-POT®** slow cooker to HIGH. Add scallops. Cook on HIGH 15 minutes longer or until scallops are just cooked through. Serve over pasta or rice.

Makes 4 servings

Pork Loin with Sherry and Red Onions

Cook Time: 8 to 10 hours (LOW) or 5 to 6 hours (HIGH)

3 **large red onions, thinly sliced**

1 **cup pearl onions, blanched and peeled**

2 **tablespoons unsalted butter or margarine**

2½ **pounds boneless pork loin, tied**

½ **teaspoon salt**

½ **teaspoon freshly ground black pepper**

½ **cup cooking sherry**

2 **tablespoons fresh chopped Italian parsley**

1½ **tablespoons cornstarch**

2 **tablespoons water**

1. Cook the red onions and pearl onions in the butter in medium skillet until soft.

2. Rub the pork loin with salt and pepper and place in 4½-quart **CROCK-POT®** slow cooker. Add the cooked onions, sherry and parsley. Cover; cook on LOW 8 to 10 hours or on HIGH for 5 to 6 hours.

3. Remove the pork loin from the stoneware; let stand 15 minutes before slicing.

4. Combine the cornstarch and water and add to the juice in the stoneware to thicken the sauce. Serve the pork loin with the onions and sherry sauce.

Makes 8 servings

Note: The mild flavor of pork is awakened by this rich, delectable sauce.

Tip: If using the 5, 6 or 7-quart **CROCK-POT®** slow cooker, double all ingredients, except for the sherry, cornstarch and water.

Hearty Beef Short Ribs

Cook Time: 8 to 9 hours (LOW) or 5½ to 6 hours (HIGH)

2½ **pounds beef short ribs, bone-in**

1 **to 2 tablespoons coarse salt**

1 **to 2 tablespoons black pepper**

2 **tablespoons olive oil, divided**

2 **carrots, cut into ¼-inch dice**

2 **celery stalks, cut into ¼-inch dice**

1 **large yellow onion, cut into ¼-inch dice**

3 **cloves garlic, minced**

3 **bay leaves**

⅓ **cup red wine**

⅓ **cup crushed tomatoes**

⅓ **cup balsamic vinegar**

1. Season ribs with salt and black pepper. Drizzle with 1 tablespoon olive oil. Heat 1 tablespoon olive oil in large skillet. Cook ribs until just browned, about 2 to 3 minutes per side. Transfer ribs to 4½-quart **CROCK-POT®** slow cooker. Add carrots, celery, onion, garlic and bay leaves.

2. Combine wine, tomatoes and vinegar in small bowl. Season with salt and black pepper, if desired. Pour mixture into **CROCK-POT®** slow cooker. Cover; cook on LOW 8 to 9 hours or HIGH 5½ to 6 hours, turning once or twice, until meat is tender and falling off the bone.

3. Remove ribs from **CROCK-POT®** slow cooker. Process sauce in blender to desired consistency. To serve, pour sauce over ribs.

Makes 6 to 8 servings

Tip: To make cleanup easier, spray the inside of the **CROCK-POT®** slow cooker with nonstick cooking spray before adding the food.

Chicken Sausage with Peppers & Basil

Cook Time: 2½ to 3 hours (HIGH)

1 **tablespoon olive oil**

1 **clove garlic, minced**

½ **yellow onion, minced (about ½ cup)**

1 **pound sweet or hot Italian chicken sausage**

1 **can (28 ounces) whole tomatoes, drained and seeded**

½ **red bell pepper, cut into ½-inch slices**

½ **yellow bell pepper, cut into ½-inch slices**

½ **orange bell pepper, cut into ½-inch slices**

¾ **cup chopped fresh basil**

Crushed red pepper flakes, to taste

Salt and black pepper, to taste

Hot cooked pasta

1. Heat oil in large skillet over medium heat until hot. Add garlic and onion, and cook until translucent.

2. Remove sausage from casing and cut into 1-inch chunks. Add to skillet and cook 3 to 4 minutes or until just beginning to brown. Transfer to 4½-quart **CROCK-POT®** slow cooker with slotted spoon, skimming off some fat.

3. Add tomatoes, bell peppers, basil, pepper flakes, salt and black pepper to **CROCK-POT®** slow cooker and stir to blend. Cook on HIGH 2½ to 3 hours or until peppers have softened. Adjust seasonings to taste. Serve over pasta.

Makes 4 servings

Paella

Cook Time: 6¼ hours (LOW) or 2¼ to 4¼ hours (HIGH)

4 cups boneless skinless chicken breasts, cut into 1-inch cubes

1 cup chopped onion

1 cup chopped tomatoes

4 teaspoons chopped pimentos

1 teaspoon salt

1 teaspoon black pepper

½ teaspoon dried oregano

¼ teaspoon saffron

4 cups cooked rice

4 cups shucked whole clams or canned clams

1 pound shrimp, peeled, deveined and cleaned

1 cup or 2 cans (8 ounces each) lobster meat

8 ounces scallops

1. Place chicken, onion, tomatoes, pimentos, salt, pepper, oregano and saffron in **CROCK-POT®** slow cooker. Cover; cook on LOW 6 hours or on HIGH 2 to 4 hours.

2. Add rice, clams, shrimp, lobster and scallops. Cover; cook on HIGH 15 minutes longer, or until shrimp are pink and firm.

Makes 8 servings

Fresh Herbed Turkey Breast

Cook Time: 8 to 10 hours (LOW) or 4 to 5 hours (HIGH)

2   **tablespoons butter, softened**

¼   **cup fresh sage leaves, minced**

¼   **cup fresh tarragon leaves, minced**

1   **clove garlic, minced**

1   **teaspoon black pepper**

½   **teaspoon salt**

1   **(4 -pound) split turkey breast**

1½   **tablespoons cornstarch**

1. Mix together the butter, sage, tarragon, garlic, pepper and salt. Rub the butter mixture all over the turkey breast.

2. Place the turkey breast in 4½-quart **CROCK-POT®** slow cooker. Cover; cook on LOW for 8 to 10 hours or on HIGH for 4 to 5 hours or until turkey is no longer pink in the center.

3. Remove the turkey breast from the stoneware. Turn the slow cooker to HIGH; slowly whisk in the cornstarch to thicken the juices. When the sauce is thick and smooth, pour over the turkey breast. Slice to serve.

Makes 8 servings

Note: Fresh herbs enliven this simple, excellent main dish.

Tip: For 5, 6 or 7-quart **CROCK-POT®** slow cooker, double all ingredients.

Cashew Chicken

Cook Time: 6 to 8 hours (LOW) or 4 to 6 hours (HIGH)

6 **boneless skinless chicken breasts**

1½ **cups cashews**

1 **cup sliced mushrooms**

1 **cup sliced celery**

1 **can (10¾ ounces) condensed cream of mushroom soup**

¼ **cup chopped green onion**

2 **tablespoons butter**

1½ **tablespoons soy sauce**
Hot cooked rice

Combine chicken, cashews, mushrooms, celery, soup, onion, butter and soy sauce in **CROCK-POT®** slow cooker. Cover; cook on LOW 6 to 8 hours or on HIGH 4 to 6 hours or until done. Serve over rice.

Helpful Hints: Time spent in the kitchen cooking with your kids is time well spent. You can share the value of preparing wholesome, comforting, nurturing foods while equipping them with the skills to create their own food traditions in the future. Even young children can participate in family meal preparation. Just remember these basics: Always make sure children are well-supervised in the kitchen. Only adults should use sharp utensils, plug in or turn on electric appliances or handle hot foods. Be sure to only assign tasks that the child can do and feel good about.

Makes 6 servings

side dishes

Gratin Potatoes with Asiago Cheese

Cook Time: 7 to 9 hours (LOW) or 5 to 6 hours (HIGH)

6 **slices bacon, cut into 1-inch pieces**

6 **medium baking potatoes, peeled and thinly sliced**

½ **cup grated Asiago cheese**

Salt and black pepper, to taste

1½ **cups heavy cream**

1. Heat skillet over medium heat until hot. Add bacon. Cook and stir until crispy. Transfer to paper towel-lined plate with slotted spoon to drain.

2. Pour bacon fat from skillet into 5- to 6-quart **CROCK-POT®** slow cooker. Layer one fourth of potatoes on bottom of **CROCK-POT®** slow cooker. Sprinkle one fourth of bacon over potatoes and top with one fourth of cheese. Add salt and pepper. Repeat layers. Pour cream over all. Cover; cook on LOW 7 to 9 hours or on HIGH 5 to 6 hours. Adjust salt and pepper, if desired.

Makes 4 to 6 servings

Arroz Con Queso

Cook Time: 6 to 9 hours (LOW)

1 **can (16 ounces) whole tomatoes, crushed**

1 **can (15 ounces) black beans, rinsed and drained**

1½ **cups uncooked long-grain converted rice**

1 **onion, chopped**

1 **cup cottage cheese**

1 **can (4 ounces) chopped green chilies**

2 **tablespoons vegetable oil**

3 **teaspoons minced garlic**

2 **cups grated Monterey Jack cheese, divided**

Combine tomatoes, beans, rice, onion, cottage cheese, chilies, oil, garlic and 1 cup cheese in 4½-quart **CROCK-POT®** slow cooker; mix thoroughly. Cover; cook on LOW 6 to 9 hours or until liquid is absorbed. Sprinkle with remaining cheese before serving.

Makes 8 to 10 servings

Boston Baked Beans

Cook Time: 10 to 12 hours (LOW) or 6 to 8 hours (HIGH)

2	**pounds small dry white beans**
12	**cups water**
	Olive oil
¼	**cup finely chopped salt pork or thick-sliced bacon**
1	**cup molasses**
½	**cup chopped onions**
½	**cup packed dark brown sugar**
2	**tablespoons dry mustard**
2	**teaspoons salt**

1. Soak beans in water in uncovered 5-quart **CROCK-POT®** slow cooker overnight (or a minimum of 8 hours). After soaking, cover; cook on LOW 3 hours. Drain liquid, reserving 1 cup. Remove beans; set aside

2. Heat oil in skillet over medium heat until hot. Add salt pork. Cook and stir 5 to 10 minutes to render fat. Remove with slotted spoon and drain on paper towels. Transfer to **CROCK-POT®** slow cooker

3. Add reserved 1 cup cooking liquid, beans, and remaining ingredients, and stir well to combine. Cover; cook on LOW 10 to 12 hours or on HIGH 6 to 8 hours.

Makes 8 servings

Wild Rice with Fruit & Nuts

Cook Time: 7 hours (LOW) or 2½ to 3 hours (HIGH)

2   **cups wild rice (or wild rice blend), rinsed***

½   **cup dried cranberries**

½   **cup chopped raisins**

½   **cup chopped dried apricots**

½   **cup almond slivers, toasted****

5   **to 6 cups chicken broth**

1   **cup orange juice**

2   **tablespoons butter, melted**

1   **teaspoon ground cumin**

2   **green onions, thinly sliced**

2   **to 3 tablespoons chopped fresh parsley**

Salt and black pepper, to taste

*Do not use parboiled rice or a blend containing parboiled rice.

**To toast almonds, spread in single layer in heavy-bottomed skillet. Cook over medium heat 1 to 2 minutes, stirring frequently, until nuts are lightly browned. Remove from skillet immediately. Cool before using.

1. Combine wild rice, cranberries, raisins, apricots and almonds in **CROCK-POT®** slow cooker.

2. Combine broth, orange juice, butter and cumin in medium bowl. Pour mixture over rice and stir to mix.

3. Cover; cook on LOW 7 hours or on HIGH 2½ to 3 hours. Stir once, adding more hot broth if necessary.

4. When rice is soft, add green onions and parsley. Adjust seasonings, if desired. Cook 10 minutes longer and serve.

Makes 6 to 8 servings

Mediterranean Red Potatoes

Cook Time: 7 to 8 hours (LOW)

3 **medium red potatoes, cut into bite-size pieces**

⅔ **cup fresh or frozen pearl onions**

Garlic-flavored cooking spray

¾ **teaspoon Italian seasoning**

¼ **teaspoon black pepper**

1 **small tomato, seeded and chopped**

2 **ounces (½ cup) crumbled feta cheese**

2 **tablespoons chopped black olives**

1. Place potatoes and onions in 1½-quart soufflé dish. Spray potatoes and onions with cooking spray; toss to coat. Add Italian seasoning and pepper; mix well. Cover dish tightly with foil.

2. Tear off 3 (18×3-inch) strips of heavy-duty foil. Cross strips to resemble wheel spokes. Place soufflé dish in center of strips. Pull foil strips up and over dish to make handles and place dish into **CROCK-POT®** slow cooker.

3. Pour hot water into **CROCK-POT®** slow cooker to about 1½ inches from top of soufflé dish. Cover; cook on LOW 7 to 8 hours.

4. Use foil handles to lift dish out of slow cooker. Stir tomato, feta cheese and olives into potato mixture.

Makes 4 servings

Macaroni and Cheese

Cook Time: 2 to 3 hours (HIGH)

6 **cups cooked macaroni**
2 **tablespoons butter**
4 **cups evaporated milk**
6 **cups (24 ounces) shredded Cheddar cheese**
2 **teaspoons salt**
½ **teaspoon black pepper**

In large mixing bowl, toss macaroni with butter. Stir in evaporated milk, cheese, salt and pepper; place in 4½-quart **CROCK-POT®** slow cooker. Cover; cook on HIGH 2 to 3 hours.

Makes 6 to 8 servings

Tip: Make this mac 'n' cheese recipe more fun. Add some tasty mix-ins: diced green or red bell pepper, peas, hot dog slices, chopped tomato, browned ground beef, chopped onion. Be creative!

Herbed Fall Vegetables

Cook Time: 4½ hours (LOW) or 3 hours (HIGH)

2 medium Yukon gold potatoes, peeled and cut into ½-inch dice

2 medium sweet potatoes, peeled and cut into ½-inch dice

3 parsnips, peeled and cut into ½-inch dice

1 medium head of fennel, sliced and cut into ½-inch dice

½ to ¾ cup chopped fresh herbs, such as tarragon, parsley, sage or thyme

4 tablespoons (½ stick) butter, cut into small pieces

1 cup chicken broth

1 tablespoon Dijon mustard

1 tablespoon salt

Freshly ground black pepper to taste

1. Combine potatoes, parsnips, fennel, herbs and butter in 4½-quart **CROCK-POT®** slow cooker.

2. Whisk together broth, mustard, salt and pepper in small bowl. Pour mixture over vegetables. Cover; cook on LOW 4½ hours or on HIGH 3 hours or until vegetables are tender, stirring occasionally to ensure even cooking.

Makes 6 servings

Creamy Curried Spinach

Cook Time: 3 to 4 hours (LOW) or 2 hours (HIGH)

3   packages (10 ounces each) frozen spinach, thawed

1   onion, chopped

4   teaspoons minced garlic

2   tablespoons curry powder

2   tablespoons butter, melted

¼   cup chicken broth

¼   cup heavy cream

1   teaspoon lemon juice

Combine spinach, onion, garlic, curry powder, butter and broth in **CROCK-POT®** slow cooker. Cover; cook on LOW 3 to 4 hours or on HIGH 2 hours or until done. Stir in cream and lemon juice 30 minutes before end of cooking time.

Makes 6 to 8 servings

Cheesy Broccoli Casserole

Cook Time: 5 to 6 hours (LOW) or 2½ to 3 hours (HIGH)

2 packages (10 ounces each) frozen chopped broccoli, thawed

1 can (10¾ ounces) condensed cream of celery soup, undiluted

1¼ cups shredded sharp Cheddar cheese, divided

¼ cup minced onion

½ teaspoon celery seed

1 teaspoon paprika

1 teaspoon hot pepper sauce

1 cup crushed potato chips or saltine crackers

1. Coat 4½-quart **CROCK-POT®** slow cooker with nonstick cooking spray. Combine broccoli, soup, 1 cup cheese, onion, celery seed, paprika and hot sauce in **CROCK-POT®** slow cooker; mix well. Cover; cook on LOW 5 to 6 hours or on HIGH 2½ to 3 hours, or until done.

2. Uncover; sprinkle top with potato chips and remaining ¼ cup cheese. Cook, uncovered, on LOW 30 to 60 minutes or on HIGH 15 to 30 minutes, or until cheese melts.

Tip: For a change in taste, prepare with thawed chopped spinach instead of broccoli, and top with crushed crackers or spicy croutons to complement the cheesy crust.

Makes 4 to 6 servings

Orange-Spiced Sweet Potatoes

Cook Time: 4 hours (LOW) or 2 hours (HIGH)

2 **pounds sweet potatoes, peeled and diced**

½ **cup packed dark brown sugar**

½ **cup (1 stick) butter, cut into small pieces**

1 **teaspoon ground cinnamon**

½ **teaspoon ground nutmeg**

½ **teaspoon grated orange peel**

Juice of 1 medium orange

¼ **teaspoon salt**

1 **teaspoon vanilla**

Chopped toasted pecans (optional)

Place all ingredients, except pecans, in **CROCK-POT®** slow cooker. Cover; cook on LOW 4 hours or on HIGH 2 hours or until potatoes are tender. Sprinkle with pecans before serving, if desired.

Makes 8 servings

Tip: For a creamy variation, mash potatoes with a hand masher or electric mixer, and add ¼ cup milk or whipping cream for moist consistency. Sprinkle with cinnamon-sugar, and sprinkle on toasted pecans, if desired.

desserts

Gingerbread

Cook Time: 1½ to 1¾ hours (HIGH)

½ **cup (1 stick) butter, softened**

½ **cup sugar**

1 **egg, lightly beaten**

1 **cup light molasses**

2½ **cups all-purpose flour**

1½ **teaspoons baking soda**

1 **teaspoon ground cinnamon**

2 **teaspoons ground ginger**

½ **teaspoon ground cloves**

½ **teaspoon salt**

1 **cup hot water**

Whipped cream (optional)

1. Coat 4½-quart **CROCK-POT®** slow cooker with butter or nonstick cooking spray. Beat together butter and sugar in large bowl. Add egg, molasses, flour, baking soda, cinnamon, ginger, cloves and salt. Stir in hot water and mix well. Pour batter into **CROCK-POT®** slow cooker.

2. Cover; cook on HIGH 1½ to 1¾ hours, or until toothpick inserted into center of cake comes out clean. Serve warm; top with whipped cream, if desired.

Makes 6 to 8 servings

Caramel and Apple Pound Cake

Cook Time: 7 to 9 hours (LOW) or 4 to 5 hours (HIGH)

4 **medium baking apples, cored, peeled and cut into wedges**

½ **cup apple juice**

½ **pound caramels, unwrapped**

¼ **cup creamy peanut butter**

1½ **teaspoons vanilla**

½ **teaspoon ground cinnamon**

⅛ **teaspoon ground cardamon**

1 **prepared pound cake, sliced**

1. Coat inside of **CROCK-POT®** slow cooker with nonstick cooking spray. Layer apples, apple juice and caramels in **CROCK-POT®** slow cooker.

2. Mix together peanut butter, vanilla, cinnamon and cardamom in small bowl. Drop by teaspoons onto apples. Cover; cook on LOW 6 to 8 hours or on HIGH 3 to 4 hours.

3. Stir thoroughly, and cook 1 hour longer. To serve, spoon warm over cake slices.

Makes 6 to 8 servings

Fudge and Cream Pudding Cake

Cook Time: 2 hours (HIGH)

2 tablespoons unsalted butter

1 cup all-purpose flour

¾ cup packed light brown sugar

5 tablespoons unsweetened cocoa powder, divided

2 teaspoons baking powder

½ teaspoon ground cinnamon

⅛ teaspoon salt

1 cup light cream

1 tablespoon vegetable oil

1 teaspoon vanilla

¾ cup packed dark brown sugar

1¾ cups hot water

Whipped cream or ice cream (optional)

1. Coat inside of 4½-quart **CROCK-POT®** slow cooker with butter. Combine flour, light brown sugar, 3 tablespoons cocoa, baking powder, cinnamon and salt in medium bowl. Add cream, oil and vanilla; stir well to combine. Pour batter into **CROCK-POT®** slow cooker.

2. Combine dark brown sugar and remaining 2 tablespoons cocoa in medium bowl. Add hot water; stir well to combine. Pour sauce over cake batter. Do not stir. Cover; cook on HIGH 2 hours.

3. Spoon portions of pudding cake onto plate. Serve with whipped cream, if desired.

Makes 8 to 10 servings

Cinnamon-Ginger Poached Pears

Cook Time: 4 to 6 hours (LOW) or 1½ to 2 hours (HIGH)

3 **cups water**

1 **cup sugar**

10 **slices fresh ginger**

2 **whole cinnamon sticks**

1 **tablespoon chopped candied ginger (optional)**

6 **Bosc or Anjou pears, peeled and cored**

1. Combine water, sugar, ginger, cinnamon and candied ginger, if desired, in 4½-quart **CROCK-POT®** slow cooker. Add pears. Cover; cook on LOW 4 to 6 hours or on HIGH 1½ to 2 hours.

2. Remove pears. Cook syrup, uncovered, 30 minutes or until thickened.

Makes 6 servings

Pineapple Rice Pudding

Cook Time: 3 to 4 hours (HIGH)

1   **can (20 ounces) crushed pineapple in juice, undrained**

1   **can (13½ ounces) coconut milk**

1   **can (12 ounces) fat-free evaporated milk**

¾   **cup uncooked arborio rice**

2   **eggs, lightly beaten**

¼   **cup granulated sugar**

¼   **cup packed light brown sugar**

½   **teaspoon ground cinnamon**

¼   **teaspoon ground nutmeg**

¼   **teaspoon salt**

Toasted coconut* and pineapple slices (optional)

*To toast coconut, spread evenly on ungreased baking sheet. Toast in preheated 350°F oven 5 to 7 minutes, stirring occasionally, until light golden brown.

1. Place pineapple with juice, coconut milk, evaporated milk, rice, eggs, sugar, brown sugar, cinnamon, nutmeg and salt into **CROCK-POT®** slow cooker; mix well. Cover; cook on high 3 to 4 hours or until thickened and rice is tender.

2. Stir until blended. Serve warm or chilled. Garnish with toasted coconut and pineapple, if desired.

Makes 8 servings

Classic Baked Apples

Cook Time: 7 to 9 hours (LOW) or 2½ to 3½ hours (HIGH)

¼ **cup packed dark brown sugar**

2 **tablespoons golden raisins**

1 **teaspoon grated lemon peel**

6 **small to medium baking apples, washed and cored**

1 **teaspoon ground cinnamon**

2 **tablespoons butter, cut into small pieces**

¼ **cup orange juice**

¼ **cup water**

Whipped cream (optional)

1. Combine brown sugar, raisins and lemon peel in small bowl. Fill core of each apple with mixture. Place apples in 4½-quart **CROCK-POT®** slow cooker. Sprinkle with cinnamon and dot with butter. Pour orange juice and water over apples. Cover; cook on LOW 7 to 9 hours or on HIGH 2½ to 3½ hours.

2. To serve, place apples in individual bowls. Top with sauce. Garnish with whipped cream, if desired.

Makes 4 serving

Triple Delicious Hot Chocolate

Cook Time: 2 hours and 10 minutes (LOW)

⅓ **cup sugar**

¼ **cup unsweetened cocoa powder**

¼ **teaspoon salt**

3 **cups milk, divided**

¾ **teaspoon vanilla**

1 **cup heavy cream**

1 **square (1 ounce) bittersweet chocolate**

1 **square (1 ounce) white chocolate**

¾ **cup whipped cream**

6 **teaspoons mini chocolate chips or shaved bittersweet chocolate**

1. Combine sugar, cocoa, salt and ½ cup milk in medium bowl. Beat until smooth. Transfer to 4½-quart **CROCK-POT®** slow cooker. Add remaining 2½ cups milk and vanilla; stir in. Cover; cook on LOW 2 hours.

2. Add cream. Cover; cook on LOW 10 minutes. Stir in bittersweet and white chocolates until melted.

3. Pour hot chocolate into 6 coffee cups. Top each serving with 2 tablespoons whipped cream and 1 teaspoon chocolate chips.

Makes 6 servings

Mulled Apple Cider

Cook Time: 2½ to 3 hours (HIGH)

2 quarts bottled apple cider or juice (not unfiltered)

¼ cup packed light brown sugar

1 square (8 inches) double-thickness cheesecloth

8 allspice berries

4 cinnamon sticks, broken into halves

12 whole cloves

1 large orange

Additional cinnamon sticks (optional)

1. Combine apple cider and brown sugar in 4½-quart **CROCK-POT®** slow cooker.

2. Rinse cheesecloth; squeeze out water. Wrap allspice berries and cinnamon stick halves in cheesecloth; tie securely with cotton string or strip of cheesecloth.

3. Stick cloves randomly into orange; cut orange into quarters. Place spice bag and orange quarters in cider mixture. Cover; cook on HIGH 2½ to 3 hours.

4. Once cooked, **CROCK-POT®** slow cooker may be turned to LOW to keep cider warm up to 3 additional hours. Remove and discard spice bag and orange before serving. Ladle cider into mugs. Garnish with additional cinnamon sticks, if desired.

Makes 10 servings

Tip: To make inserting cloves into the orange a little easier, first pierce the orange skin with the point of wooden skewer. Remove the skewer and insert a clove.

VOLUME MEASUREMENTS (dry)

$1/8$ teaspoon = 0.5 mL
$1/4$ teaspoon = 1 mL
$1/2$ teaspoon = 2 mL
$3/4$ teaspoon = 4 mL
1 teaspoon = 5 mL
1 tablespoon = 15 mL
2 tablespoons = 30 mL
$1/4$ cup = 60 mL
$1/3$ cup = 75 mL
$1/2$ cup = 125 mL
$2/3$ cup = 150 mL
$3/4$ cup = 175 mL
1 cup = 250 mL
2 cups = 1 pint = 500 mL
3 cups = 750 mL
4 cups = 1 quart = 1 L

VOLUME MEASUREMENTS (fluid)

1 fluid ounce (2 tablespoons) = 30 mL
4 fluid ounces ($1/2$ cup) = 125 mL
8 fluid ounces (1 cup) = 250 mL
12 fluid ounces ($1 1/2$ cups) = 375 mL
16 fluid ounces (2 cups) = 500 mL

WEIGHTS (mass)

$1/2$ ounce = 15 g
1 ounce = 30 g
3 ounces = 90 g
4 ounces = 120 g
8 ounces = 225 g
10 ounces = 285 g
12 ounces = 360 g
16 ounces = 1 pound = 450 g

DIMENSIONS

$1/16$ inch = 2 mm
$1/8$ inch = 3 mm
$1/4$ inch = 6 mm
$1/2$ inch = 1.5 cm
$3/4$ inch = 2 cm
1 inch = 2.5 cm

OVEN TEMPERATURES

250°F = 120°C
275°F = 140°C
300°F = 150°C
325°F = 160°C
350°F = 180°C
375°F = 190°C
400°F = 200°C
425°F = 220°C
450°F = 230°C

BAKING PAN SIZES

Utensil	Size in Inches/Quarts	Metric Volume	Size in Centimeters
Baking or	8×8×2	2 L	20×20×5
Cake Pan	9×9×2	2.5 L	23×23×5
(square or	12×8×2	3 L	30×20×5
rectangular)	13×9×2	3.5 L	33×23×5
Loaf Pan	8×4×3	1.5 L	20×10×7
	9×5×3	2 L	23×13×7
Round Layer	8×1½	1.2 L	20×4
Cake Pan	9×1½	1.5 L	23×4
Pie Plate	8×1¼	750 mL	20×3
	9×1¼	1 L	23×3
Baking Dish	1 quart	1 L	—
or Casserole	1½ quarts	1.5 L	—
	2 quarts	2 L	—

Maple-Glazed Meatballs

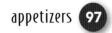

Warm Blue Crab Bruschetta

Maple-Glazed Meatballs

1½ cups ketchup
1 cup maple syrup or maple-flavored syrup
⅓ cup reduced-sodium soy sauce
1 tablespoon quick-cooking tapioca
1½ teaspoons ground allspice
1 teaspoon dry mustard
2 packages (about 16 ounces each) frozen fully cooked meatballs, partially thawed and separated
1 can (20 ounces) pineapple chunks in juice, drained

Cook Time: 5 to 6 hours (LOW)

1. Combine ketchup, maple syrup, soy sauce, tapioca, allspice and mustard in 4½-quart **CROCK-POT®** slow cooker.

2. Carefully stir meatballs and pineapple chunks into ketchup mixture.

3. Cover; cook on LOW 5 to 6 hours. Stir before serving. Serve warm; insert cocktail picks, if desired.

Makes about 48 meatballs

Tip: For a quick main dish, serve meatballs over hot cooked rice.

Warm Blue Crab Bruschetta

4 cups peeled, seeded and diced Roma or plum tomatoes
1 cup diced white onion
2 teaspoons minced garlic
⅓ cup olive oil
2 tablespoons balsamic vinegar
½ teaspoon dried oregano
2 tablespoons sugar
1 pound lump blue crabmeat, picked over for shells
1½ teaspoons kosher salt
½ teaspoon cracked black pepper
⅓ cup minced fresh basil
2 baguettes, sliced and toasted

Cook Time: 3 hours (LOW)

1. Combine tomatoes, onion, garlic, oil, vinegar, oregano and sugar in 4½-quart **CROCK-POT®** slow cooker. Cover; cook on LOW 2 hours.

2. Add crabmeat, salt and pepper. Stir gently to mix, taking care not to break up crabmeat lumps. Cook on LOW 1 hour.

3. Fold in basil. Serve on toasted baguette slices.

Makes 16 servings

Serving Suggestion: Crab topping can also be served on Melba toast or whole-grain crackers.

Sausage and Swiss Chard Stuffed Mushrooms

Honey-Glazed Chicken Wings

Sausage and Swiss Chard Stuffed Mushrooms

2 packages (6 ounces each) large mushrooms,* wiped clean

4 tablespoons extra-virgin olive oil, divided

½ pound bulk pork sausage

½ onion, finely chopped

2 cups chopped Swiss chard, rinsed

¼ teaspoon dried thyme

2 tablespoons garlic-and-herb-flavored dried bread crumbs

1½ cups chicken broth, divided

Salt and black pepper

2 tablespoons grated Parmesan cheese

2 tablespoons chopped fresh parsley

Use "baby bellas" or cremini mushrooms. Do not substitute white button mushrooms.

Cook Time: 3 hours (HIGH)

1. Coat inside of 5- to 6-quart **CROCK-POT®** slow cooker with nonstick cooking spray. Remove stems from mushrooms and hollow out caps. Brush inside and out using 3 tablespoons oil.

2. Heat remaining 1 tablespoon oil in medium skillet over medium heat. Crumble sausage into skillet and cook until browned. Transfer to medium bowl with slotted spoon.

3. Return skillet to heat. Add onion and cook until translucent. Stir in chard and thyme and cook just until chard wilts. Remove from heat. Stir in cooked sausage, bread crumbs and 1 tablespoon broth. Season with salt and pepper. Divide evenly among mushroom caps.

4. Pour remaining broth into **CROCK-POT®** slow cooker. Arrange mushrooms in broth. Cover; cook on HIGH 3 hours or until tender. Sprinkle with cheese and parsley before serving.

Makes 6 to 8 servings

Variation: If desired, place a small square of sliced Swiss cheese on each mushroom and continue cooking 15 minutes longer or until cheese is melted. Proceed as directed.

Honey-Glazed Chicken Wings

3 tablespoons vegetable oil, divided

3 pounds chicken wings, tips removed

1 cup honey

½ cup soy sauce

1 clove garlic, minced

2 tablespoons tomato paste

2 teaspoons water

1 teaspoon sugar

1 teaspoon black pepper

Cook Time: 6 to 8 hours (LOW) or 3 to 4 hours (HIGH)

1. Heat 1½ tablespoons oil in skillet over medium heat until hot. Brown chicken wings on each side in batches to prevent crowding. Turn each piece as it browns, about 1 to 2 minutes per side. Transfer with slotted spoon to **CROCK-POT®** slow cooker.

2. Combine honey, soy sauce, remaining 1½ tablespoons vegetable oil, and garlic in medium bowl. Whisk in tomato paste, water, sugar and pepper. Pour sauce over chicken. Cover; cook on LOW 6 to 8 hours or on HIGH 3 to 4 hours.

Makes 6 to 8 servings

Refried Bean Dip with Blue Tortilla Chips

Creamy Artichoke-Parmesan Dip

Refried Bean Dip with Blue Tortilla Chips

3 cans (16 ounces each) refried beans

1 cup prepared taco sauce

½ teaspoon salt

½ teaspoon black pepper

3 cups shredded Cheddar cheese, divided

¾ cup chopped green onions

2 packages (12 ounces each) blue tortilla chips

Cook Time: 2 to 4 hours (LOW)

Combine refried beans, taco sauce, salt and pepper in large bowl. Spread one-third of bean mixture on bottom of 4½-quart **CROCK-POT®** slow cooker. Sprinkle evenly with ¾ cup cheese. Repeat layers, finishing with cheese layer. Sprinkle green onions evenly on cheese. Cover; cook on LOW 2 to 4 hours. Serve with blue tortilla chips for dipping.

Makes 10 servings

Creamy Artichoke-Parmesan Dip

2 cans (14 ounces each) artichoke hearts, drained and chopped

2 cups (8 ounces) shredded mozzarella cheese

1½ cups grated Parmesan cheese

1½ cups mayonnaise

½ cup finely chopped onion

½ teaspoon dried oregano

¼ teaspoon garlic powder

4 pita breads, cut into wedges

Assorted cut-up vegetables

Cook Time: 2 hours (LOW)

Place artichokes, mozzarella cheese, Parmesan cheese, mayonnaise, onion, oregano and garlic powder in 1½-quart or other small-sized **CROCK-POT®** slow cooker; mix well. Cover; cook on LOW 2 hours. Arrange pita bread wedges and vegetables on platter; serve with warm dip.

Makes 16 servings (about 4 cups)

Tip: When adapting conventionally prepared recipes for your **CROCK-POT®** slow cooker, revise the amount of herbs and spices you use. For example, whole herbs and spices increase in flavor while ground spices tend to lose flavor during slow cooking. You can adjust the seasonings or add fresh herbs and spices just before serving the dish.

Cereal Snack Mix

Chili Con Queso

Cereal Snack Mix

6	tablespoons unsalted butter, melted
2	tablespoons curry powder
2	tablespoons reduced-sodium soy sauce
1	tablespoon sugar
1	tablespoon paprika
2	teaspoons ground cumin
½	teaspoon salt
5	cups rice squares cereal
5	cups corn squares cereal
1	cup tiny pretzels
⅓	cup lightly salted peanuts

Cook Time: 45 minutes (HIGH) plus 3 to 4 hours (LOW)

1. Pour butter in 4½-quart **CROCK·POT®** slow cooker. Stir in curry, soy sauce, sugar, paprika, cumin and salt. Stir in cereal, pretzels and peanuts. Cook, uncovered, on HIGH 45 minutes, stirring often to avoid sugar scorching.

2. Reduce **CROCK·POT®** slow cooker to LOW and cook, uncovered, 3 to 4 hours longer, stirring often. Let cool and transfer to large serving bowl.

Makes 20 servings

Chili Con Queso

1	package (16 ounces) pasteurized processed cheese spread, cubed
1	can (10 ounces) diced tomatoes with green chiles
1	cup sliced green onions
2	teaspoons ground coriander
2	teaspoons ground cumin
¾	teaspoon hot pepper sauce
	Green onion strips (optional)
	Hot pepper slices (optional)
	Tortilla chips

Cook Time: 2 to 3 hours (LOW)

1. Combine cheese spread, tomatoes, green onions, coriander and cumin in **CROCK·POT®** slow cooker; stir until well blended.

2. Cover; cook on LOW 2 to 3 hours or until hot.*

3. Garnish with green onion strips and hot pepper slices, if desired. Serve with tortilla chips.

Dip will be very hot; use caution when serving.

Makes 3 cups

Serving Suggestion: Serve Chili con Queso with tortilla chips. For something different, cut pita bread into triangles and toast them in a preheated 400°F oven for 5 minutes or until they are crisp.

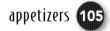

Barbecued Meatballs

Sweet and Spicy Sausage Rounds

Barbecued Meatballs

2	pounds (32 ounces) 95% lean ground beef
1⅓	cups ketchup, divided
3	tablespoons seasoned dry bread crumbs
1	egg, lightly beaten
2	tablespoons dried onion flakes
¾	teaspoon garlic salt
½	teaspoon black pepper
1	cup packed light brown sugar
1	can (6 ounces) tomato paste
¼	cup reduced-sodium soy sauce
¼	cup cider vinegar
1½	teaspoons hot pepper sauce
	Sliced green bell peppers (optional)

Cook Time: 4 hours (LOW)

1. Preheat oven to 350°F. Combine ground beef, ⅓ cup ketchup, bread crumbs, egg, onion flakes, garlic salt and black pepper in medium bowl. Mix lightly but thoroughly; shape into 1-inch meatballs.

2. Place meatballs in 2 (15×10-inch) jelly-roll pans or shallow roasting pans. Bake 18 minutes or until browned. Transfer to 4½-quart **CROCK-POT®** slow cooker.

3. Mix remaining 1 cup ketchup, sugar, tomato paste, soy sauce, vinegar and hot pepper sauce in medium bowl. Pour over meatballs. Cover; cook on LOW 4 hours. Add jalapeño slices to mixture, if desired. Serve with cocktail picks.

Makes about 4 dozen meatballs

Barbecued Franks: Arrange 2 (12-ounce) packages or 3 (8-ounce) packages cocktail franks in slow cooker. Combine 1 cup ketchup with brown sugar, tomato paste, soy sauce, vinegar and hot pepper sauce in medium bowl; pour over franks. Cook according to directions for Barbecued Meatballs.

Sweet and Spicy Sausage Rounds

1	pound kielbasa sausage, cut into ¼-inch-thick rounds
⅔	cup blackberry jam
⅓	cup steak sauce
1	tablespoon prepared yellow mustard
½	teaspoon ground allspice

Cook Time: 3 hours (HIGH)

1. Place all ingredients in **CROCK-POT®** slow cooker; toss to coat completely. Cook on HIGH 3 hours or until richly glazed.

2. Serve with decorative cocktail picks.

Makes 3 cups

Roasted Corn and Red Pepper Chowder

Northwest Beef and Vegetable Soup

Roasted Corn and Red Pepper Chowder

2   **tablespoons extra-virgin olive oil**

2   **cups fresh corn kernels or frozen corn, thawed**

1   **red bell pepper, cored, seeded and diced**

2   **green onions, sliced**

4   **cups chicken broth**

2   **baking potatoes, peeled and diced**

1   **teaspoon salt**

½   **teaspoon black pepper**

1   **can (13 ounces) evaporated milk**

2   **tablespoons minced flat-leaf parsley**

Cook Time: 7 to 9 hours (LOW) or 4 to 5 hours (HIGH)

1. Heat oil in skillet over medium heat until hot. Add corn, bell pepper and green onions. Cook and stir until vegetables are tender and lightly browned, about 7 to 8 minutes. Transfer to **CROCK-POT®** slow cooker.

2. Add broth, potatoes, salt and pepper. Stir well to combine. Cover; cook on LOW 7 to 9 hours or on HIGH 4 to 5 hours.

3. Thirty minutes before serving, add evaporated milk. Stir well to combine and continue cooking. To serve, garnish with parsley.

Makes 4 servings

Northwest Beef and Vegetable Soup

2   **tablespoons olive oil**

1   **pound lean stew beef, fat removed and cut into 1-inch cubes**

1   **medium onion, chopped**

1   **clove garlic, minced**

3½ **cups canned crushed tomatoes, undrained**

1   **can (15 ounces) white beans, drained and rinsed**

1   **buttercup squash, peeled and diced**

1   **turnip, peeled and diced**

1   **large potato, peeled and diced**

2   **stalks celery, sliced**

2   **tablespoons minced fresh basil**

1½ **teaspoons salt**

1   **teaspoon black pepper**

8   **cups water**

Cook Time: 2 hours (HIGH), plus 4 to 6 hours (LOW)

1. Heat oil in skillet over medium heat until hot. Sear beef on all sides, turning as it browns. Add onion and garlic during last few minutes of searing. Transfer to 4½-quart **CROCK-POT®** slow cooker.

2. Add remaining ingredients. Gently stir well to combine. Cover; cook on HIGH 2 hours. Turn **CROCK-POT®** slow cooker to LOW. Cook on LOW 4 to 6 hours longer, stirring occasionally and adjusting seasonings to taste.

Makes 6 to 8 servings

Mushroom Barley Stew

Cannellini Minestrone Soup

Mushroom Barley Stew

1 cup dried mushrooms

1 cup pearl barley, rinsed and sorted (about ½ pound)

1 package (10 ounces) fresh mushrooms, rinsed and thinly sliced

2 carrots, peeled and cut into ¼-inch dice

2 celery stalks, cut into ¼-inch dice

1 yellow onion, cut into ¼-inch dice

1 tablespoon fresh thyme

2 bay leaves

1 tablespoon tomato paste

Salt and black pepper, to taste

8 to 10 cups chicken or mushroom stock

2 tablespoons minced fresh parsley

Cook Time: 5½ hours (LOW) or 3 to 4 hours (HIGH)

1. Place dried mushrooms in small bowl and cover with warm water. Set aside to soak 15 minutes or until softened. Transfer mushrooms and soaking liquid (taking care to discard any grit) to 4½-quart **CROCK-POT®** slow cooker.

2. Add barley, fresh mushrooms, carrots, celery, onion, thyme, bay leaves, tomato paste, salt and black pepper. Stir to combine then pour in stock.

2. Cover; cook on LOW 5½ hours or on HIGH 3 to 4 hours, or until barley and vegetables are tender. Add additional salt and pepper to taste before serving garnished with parsley.

Makes 8 to 10 servings

Cannellini Minestrone Soup

4 cups chicken broth

1 can (14½ ounces) diced tomatoes, undrained

1 can (12 ounces) tomato-vegetable juice

2 cups escarole, cut into ribbons

1 cup chopped green onions

1 cup chopped carrots

1 cup chopped celery

1 cup chopped potatoes

¼ cup dried cannellini beans, sorted and rinsed

2 tablespoons chopped fresh chives

1 tablespoon chopped fresh flat-leaf parsley

¼ teaspoon salt

¼ teaspoon black pepper

2 ounces uncooked ditalini pasta

Cook Time: 6 to 8 hours (LOW) or 4 to 6 hours (HIGH)

1. Place all ingredients except pasta, in 5-quart **CROCK-POT®** slow cooker. Stir well to combine. Cover; cook on LOW 6 to 8 hours or on HIGH 4 to 6 hours.

2. Add ditalini and stir again. Cover; cook 20 minutes before serving.

Makes 6 servings

Chicken Tortilla Soup

Best Ever Chili

Chicken Tortilla Soup

4   boneless skinless chicken
     thighs
2   cans (15 ounces each)
     diced tomatoes,
     undrained
1   can (4 ounces) chopped
     mild green chilies,
     drained
½   to 1 cup chicken broth
1   yellow onion, diced
2   cloves of garlic, minced
1   teaspoon ground cumin
     Salt and black pepper
4   corn tortillas, sliced into
     ¼-inch strips and baked
     until crisp
2   tablespoons chopped
     fresh cilantro
½   cup shredded Monterey
     Jack cheese
1   avocado, peeled, diced
     and tossed with lime
     juice
     Lime wedges

Cook Time: 6 hours (LOW) or 3 hours (HIGH)

1. Place chicken in 4½-quart **CROCK-POT®** slow cooker. Combine tomatoes with juice, chilies, ½ cup broth, onion, garlic and cumin in small bowl. Pour mixture over chicken.

2. Cover; cook on LOW 6 hours or on HIGH 3 hours, or until chicken is tender. Remove chicken from **CROCK-POT®** slow cooker. Shred with 2 forks. Return to cooking liquid. Adjust seasonings, adding salt and pepper and more broth, if necessary.

3. Just before serving, add tortillas and cilantro to **CROCK-POT®** slow cooker. Stir to blend. Serve in soup bowls, topping each serving with cheese, avocado and a squeeze of lime juice.

Makes 4 to 6 servings

Best Ever Chili

1½   pounds ground beef
1   cup chopped onion
2   cans (about 15 ounces
     each) kidney beans,
     drained, canning liquid
     reserved
1½   pounds plum tomatoes,
     diced
1   can (15 ounces) tomato
     paste
3   to 6 tablespoons chili
     powder

Cook Time: 10 to 12 hours (LOW)

1. Cook and stir beef and onion in large skillet over medium-high heat, stirring to break up meat, 10 minutes or until meat is no longer pink. Drain; transfer beef mixture to slow cooker.

2. Add kidney beans, tomatoes, tomato paste, 1 cup reserved bean canning liquid and chili powder to 4½-quart **CROCK-POT®** slow cooker; mix well. Cover; cook on LOW 10 to 12 hours or until tomatoes have softened completely.

Makes 8 serving:

Chipotle Chicken Stew

Manhattan Clam Chowder

Chipotle Chicken Stew

1 pound boneless skinless chicken thighs, cut into cubes

1 can (15 ounces) navy beans, rinsed and drained

1 can (15 ounces) black beans, rinsed and drained

1 can (14½ ounces) crushed tomatoes, undrained

1½ cups chicken broth

½ cup orange juice

1 medium onion, diced

1 chipotle pepper in adobo sauce, minced

1 teaspoon salt

1 teaspoon ground cumin

1 bay leaf

Cilantro sprigs (optional)

Cook Time: 7 to 8 hours (LOW) or 3½ to 4 hours (HIGH)

1. Combine chicken, beans, tomatoes with juice, broth, orange juice, onion, chipotle pepper, salt, cumin and bay leaf in 4½-quart **CROCK-POT®** slow cooker.

2. Cover; cook on LOW 7 to 8 hours or on HIGH 3½ to 4 hours. Remove bay leaf before serving. Garnish with cilantro sprigs, if desired.

Makes 6 servings

Manhattan Clam Chowder

3 slices bacon, diced

2 stalks celery, chopped

3 onions, chopped

2 cups water

1 can (15 ounces) stewed tomatoes, undrained and chopped

4 small red potatoes, diced

2 carrots, diced

½ teaspoon dried thyme

½ teaspoon black pepper

½ teaspoon Louisiana-style hot sauce

1 pound minced clams*

If fresh clams are unavailable, use canned clams; 6 (6½-ounce) cans yield about 1 pound of clam meat; drain and discard liquid.

Cook Time: 6 to 8 hours (LOW) or 4 to 6 hours (HIGH)

1. Cook and stir bacon in medium saucepan until bacon is crisp. Remove bacon and place in **CROCK-POT®** slow cooker.

2. Add celery and onions to skillet. Cook and stir until tender. Place in **CROCK-POT®** slow cooker.

3. Mix in water, tomatoes with juice, potatoes, carrots, thyme, pepper and hot sauce. Cover; cook on LOW 6 to 8 hours or HIGH 4 to 6 hours. Add clams during last half hour of cooking.

Makes 4 servings

Tip: Shellfish and mollusks are delicate and should be added to the **CROCK-POT®** slow cooker during the last 15 to 30 minutes of the cooking time if you're using the high heat setting, and during the last 30 to 45 minutes if you're using the low setting. This type of seafood overcooks easily, becoming tough and rubbery, so watch your cooking times, and cook only long enough for foods to be done.

Easy Beef Stew

Savory Chicken and Oregano Chili

Easy Beef Stew

2 **pounds beef for stew, cut into 1-inch cubes**

1 **can (4 ounces) mushrooms**

1 **envelope (1 ounce) dry onion soup mix**

⅓ **cup red or white wine**

1 **can (10 ounces) cream of mushroom soup, undiluted**

Hot cooked noodles

Cook Time: 8 to 12 hours (LOW)

Combine all ingredients, except noodles, in **CROCK-POT®** slow cooker. Cover; cook on LOW 8 to 12 hours. Serve over noodles.

Makes 4 to 6 servings

Tip: Browning the beef before cooking it in a **CROCK-POT®** slow cooker isn't necessary but helps to enhance the flavor and appearance of the stew. If you have the time, use nonstick cooking spray and brown the meat in a large skillet before placing it in the **CROCK-POT®** slow cooker; follow the recipe as written.

Savory Chicken and Oregano Chili

3 **cans (15 ounces each) Great Northern or cannellini beans, drained**

3½ **cups chicken broth**

2 **cups chopped cooked chicken**

2 **medium red bell peppers, cored, seeded and chopped**

1 **medium onion, peeled and chopped**

1 **can (4 ounces) diced green chiles**

3 **cloves garlic, minced**

2 **teaspoons ground cumin**

1 **teaspoon salt**

1 **tablespoon minced fresh oregano**

Cook Time: 8 to 10 hours (LOW) or 4 to 5 hours (HIGH)

1. Place beans, broth, chicken, bell peppers, onion, chiles, garlic, cumin and salt in 5- to 6-quart **CROCK-POT®** slow cooker. Mix well to combine. Cover; cook on LOW 8 to 10 hours or on HIGH 4 to 5 hours.

2. Stir in oregano before serving.

Makes 8 servings

Barbecued Pulled Pork Sandwiches

Stuffed Chicken Breasts

Barbecued Pulled Pork Sandwiches

1 **(2½ pounds) pork shoulder roast**

1 **bottle (14 ounces) barbecue sauce**

1 **tablespoon fresh lemon juice**

1 **teaspoon brown sugar**

1 **medium onion, chopped**

8 **hamburger buns or hard rolls**

Cook Time: 12 to 14 hours (LOW) or 6 to 7 hours (HIGH)

1. Place the pork roast in 4½-quart **CROCK-POT®** slow cooker. Cover; cook on LOW for 10 to 12 hours or on HIGH for 5 to 6 hours.

2. Remove the pork roast from the stoneware. Shred the pork with 2 forks. Discard any liquid in the stoneware. Return the pork to the stoneware; add the barbecue sauce, lemon juice, brown sugar and onion. Cook on HIGH for 1 hour or on LOW for 2 hours.

3. Serve the pork on hamburger buns or hard rolls.

Makes 8 servings

Note: This kid-popular dish is sweet and savory, and most importantly, extremely easy to make. Serve with crunchy coleslaw on the side.

Tip: For a 5, 6 or 7-quart **CROCK-POT®** slow cooker, double all ingredients, except for the barbecue sauce. Increase the barbecue sauce to 21 ounces.

Stuffed Chicken Breasts

6 **boneless skinless chicken breasts**

8 **ounces feta cheese, crumbled**

3 **cups chopped fresh spinach leaves**

⅓ **cup oil-packed sun-dried tomatoes, drained and chopped**

1 **teaspoon minced lemon peel**

1 **teaspoon dried basil, oregano or mint**

½ **teaspoon garlic powder**
Freshly ground black pepper, to taste

1 **can (15 ounces) diced tomatoes, undrained**

½ **cup oil-cured olives***
Hot cooked polenta

*If using pitted olives, add to CROCK-POT® slow cooker in the final hour of cooking.

Cook Time: 5½ to 6 hours (LOW) or 4 hours (HIGH)

1. Place chicken breast between 2 pieces of plastic wrap. Using tenderizer mallet or back of skillet, pound breast until about ¼ inch thick. Repeat with remaining chicken.

2. Combine feta, spinach, sun-dried tomatoes, lemon peel, basil, garlic powder and pepper in medium bowl.

3. Lay pounded chicken, smooth-side down, on work surface. Place about 2 tablespoons feta mixture on wide end of breast. Roll tightly. Repeat with remaining chicken.

4. Place rolled chicken, seam-side down, in 4½-quart **CROCK-POT®** slow cooker. Top with diced tomatoes with juice and olives. Cover; cook on LOW 5½ to 6 hours or on HIGH 4 hours. Serve with polenta.

Makes 6 servings

Tex-Mex Beef Wraps

Scallops in Fresh Tomato and Herb Sauce

Tex-Mex Beef Wraps

1	**tablespoon chili powder**
2	**teaspoons ground cumin**
1	**teaspoon salt**
¼	**teaspoon ground red pepper**
1	**boneless beef chuck pot roast (2½ to 3 pounds), cut into 4 pieces**
1	**medium onion, chopped**
3	**cloves garlic, minced**
1	**cup salsa, divided**
12	**(6- to 7-inch) flour or corn tortillas, warmed**
1	**cup shredded Cheddar or Jack cheese**
1	**cup chopped tomato**
¼	**cup chopped cilantro**
1	**ripe avocado, diced**

Cook Time: 8 to 9 hours (LOW) or 3½ to 4½ hours (HIGH)

1. Blend chili powder, cumin, salt and red pepper. Rub meat all over with spice mixture. Place onion and garlic in bottom of 4½-quart **CROCK-POT®** slow cooker; top with meat. Spoon ½ cup salsa over meat. Cover and cook on LOW 8 to 9 hours, or on HIGH 3½ to 4½ hours.

2. Remove meat from **CROCK-POT®** slow cooker; place on plate and use 2 forks to shred meat. Skim off and discard fat from cooking liquid; return meat to juices and mix well. Adjust seasonings. Place meat on warm tortillas; top with cheese, tomato, cilantro and avocado. Roll up to enclose filling. Serve with remaining salsa.

Makes 6 servings

Scallops in Fresh Tomato and Herb Sauce

2	**tablespoons vegetable oil**
1	**medium red onion, peeled and diced**
1	**clove garlic, minced**
3½	**cups fresh tomatoes, peeled***
1	**can (12 ounces) tomato purée**
1	**can (6 ounces) tomato paste**
¼	**cup dry red wine**
2	**tablespoons chopped flat-leaf parsley**
1	**tablespoon chopped fresh oregano**
¼	**teaspoon black pepper**
1½	**pounds fresh scallops, cleaned and drained**

Cook Time: 6 to 8 hours (LOW) and 15 minutes (HIGH)

1. Heat oil in skillet over medium heat until hot. Add onion and garlic. Cook and stir 7 to 8 minutes, or until onions are soft and translucent. Transfer to 4½-quart **CROCK-POT®** slow cooker.

2. Add tomatoes, tomato purée, tomato paste, wine, parsley, oregano and pepper. Cover; cook on LOW 6 to 8 hours.

3. Turn **CROCK-POT®** slow cooker to HIGH. Add scallops. Cook on HIGH 15 minutes longer or until scallops are just cooked through. Serve over pasta or rice.

Makes 4 servings

*To peel tomatoes, place one at a time in simmering water about 10 seconds. (Add 30 seconds if tomatoes are not fully ripened.) Immediately plunge into a bowl of cold water for another 10 seconds. Peel skin with a knife.

Pork Loin with Sherry and Red Onions

Hearty Beef Short Ribs

Pork Loin with Sherry and Red Onions

3	large red onions, thinly sliced
1	cup pearl onions, blanched and peeled
2	tablespoons unsalted butter or margarine
2½	pounds boneless pork loin, tied
½	teaspoon salt
½	teaspoon freshly ground black pepper
½	cup cooking sherry
2	tablespoons fresh chopped Italian parsley
1½	tablespoons cornstarch
2	tablespoons water

Cook Time: 8 to 10 hours (LOW) or 5 to 6 hours (HIGH)

1. Cook the red onions and pearl onions in the butter in medium skillet until soft.

2. Rub the pork loin with salt and pepper and place in 4½-quart **CROCK-POT®** slow cooker. Add the cooked onions, sherry and parsley. Cover; cook on LOW 8 to 10 hours or on HIGH for 5 to 6 hours.

3. Remove the pork loin from the stoneware; let stand 15 minutes before slicing.

4. Combine the cornstarch and water and add to the juice in the stoneware to thicken the sauce. Serve the pork loin with the onions and sherry sauce.

Makes 8 servings

Note: The mild flavor of pork is awakened by this rich, delectable sauce.

Tip: If using the 5, 6 or 7-quart **CROCK-POT®** slow cooker, double all ingredients, except for the sherry, cornstarch and water.

Hearty Beef Short Ribs

2½	pounds beef short ribs, bone-in
1	to 2 tablespoons coarse salt
1	to 2 tablespoons black pepper
2	tablespoons olive oil, divided
2	carrots, cut into ¼-inch dice
2	celery stalks, cut into ¼-inch dice
1	large yellow onion, cut into ¼-inch dice
3	cloves garlic, minced
3	bay leaves
⅓	cup red wine
⅓	cup crushed tomatoes
⅓	cup balsamic vinegar

Cook Time: 8 to 9 hours (LOW) or 5½ to 6 hours (HIGH)

1. Season ribs with salt and black pepper. Drizzle with 1 tablespoon olive oil. Heat 1 tablespoon olive oil in large skillet. Cook ribs until just browned, about 2 to 3 minutes per side. Transfer ribs to 4½-quart **CROCK-POT®** slow cooker. Add carrots, celery, onion, garlic and bay leaves.

2. Combine wine, tomatoes and vinegar in small bowl. Season with salt and black pepper, if desired. Pour mixture into **CROCK-POT®** slow cooker. Cover; cook on LOW 8 to 9 hours or HIGH 5½ to 6 hours, turning once or twice, until meat is tender and falling off the bone.

3. Remove ribs from **CROCK-POT®** slow cooker. Process sauce in blender to desired consistency. To serve, pour sauce over ribs.

Makes 6 to 8 servings

Tip: To make cleanup easier, spray the inside of the **CROCK-POT®** slow cooker with nonstick cooking spray before adding the food.

Chicken Sausage with Peppers & Basil

Paella

Chicken Sausage with Peppers & Basil

1 tablespoon olive oil

1 clove garlic, minced

½ yellow onion, minced (about ½ cup)

1 pound sweet or hot Italian chicken sausage

1 can (28 ounces) whole tomatoes, drained and seeded

½ red bell pepper, cut into ½-inch slices

½ yellow bell pepper, cut into ½-inch slices

½ orange bell pepper, cut into ½-inch slices

¾ cup chopped fresh basil

Crushed red pepper flakes, to taste

Salt and black pepper, to taste

Hot cooked pasta

Cook Time: 2½ to 3 hours (HIGH)

1. Heat oil in large skillet over medium heat until hot. Add garlic and onion, and cook until translucent.

2. Remove sausage from casing and cut into 1-inch chunks. Add to skillet and cook 3 to 4 minutes or until just beginning to brown. Transfer to 4½-quart **CROCK-POT®** slow cooker with slotted spoon, skimming off some fat.

3. Add tomatoes, bell peppers, basil, pepper flakes, salt and black pepper to **CROCK-POT®** slow cooker and stir to blend. Cook on HIGH 2½ to 3 hours or until peppers have softened. Adjust seasonings to taste. Serve over pasta.

Makes 4 servings

Paella

4 cups boneless skinless chicken breasts, cut into 1-inch cubes

1 cup chopped onion

1 cup chopped tomatoes

4 teaspoons chopped pimentos

1 teaspoon salt

1 teaspoon black pepper

½ teaspoon dried oregano

¼ teaspoon saffron

4 cups cooked rice

4 cups shucked whole clams or canned clams

1 pound shrimp, peeled, deveined and cleaned

1 cup or 2 cans (8 ounces each) lobster meat

8 ounces scallops

Cook Time: 6¼ hours (LOW) or 2¼ to 4¼ hours (HIGH)

1. Place chicken, onion, tomatoes, pimentos, salt, pepper, oregano and saffron in **CROCK-POT®** slow cooker. Cover; cook on LOW 6 hours or on HIGH 2 to 4 hours.

2. Add rice, clams, shrimp, lobster and scallops. Cover; cook on HIGH 15 minutes longer, or until shrimp are pink and firm.

Makes 8 servings

CROCK·POT.
THE ORIGINAL SLOW COOKER

Fresh Herbed Turkey Breast

CROCK·POT.
THE ORIGINAL SLOW COOKER

Cashew Chicken

CROCK·POT.
THE ORIGINAL SLOW COOKER

Fresh Herbed Turkey Breast

2 tablespoons butter, softened

¼ cup fresh sage leaves, minced

¼ cup fresh tarragon leaves, minced

1 clove garlic, minced

1 teaspoon black pepper

½ teaspoon salt

1 (4 -pound) split turkey breast

1½ tablespoons cornstarch

Cook Time: 8 to 10 hours (LOW) or 4 to 5 hours (HIGH)

1. Mix together the butter, sage, tarragon, garlic, pepper and salt. Rub the butter mixture all over the turkey breast.

2. Place the turkey breast in 4½-quart **CROCK-POT®** slow cooker. Cover; cook on LOW for 8 to 10 hours or on HIGH for 4 to 5 hours or until turkey is no longer pink in the center.

3. Remove the turkey breast from the stoneware. Turn the slow cooker to HIGH; slowly whisk in the cornstarch to thicken the juices. When the sauce is thick and smooth, pour over the turkey breast. Slice to serve.

Makes 8 servings

Note: Fresh herbs enliven this simple, excellent main dish.

Tip: For 5,6 or 7-quart **CROCK-POT®** slow cooker, double all ingredients.

Cashew Chicken

6 boneless skinless chicken breasts

1½ cups cashews

1 cup sliced mushrooms

1 cup sliced celery

1 can (10¾ ounces) condensed cream of mushroom soup

¼ cup chopped green onion

2 tablespoons butter

1½ tablespoons soy sauce

Hot cooked rice

Cook Time: 6 to 8 hours (LOW) or 4 to 6 hours (HIGH)

Combine chicken, cashews, mushrooms, celery, soup, onion, butter and soy sauce in **CROCK-POT®** slow cooker. Cover; cook on LOW 6 to 8 hours or on HIGH 4 to 6 hours or until done. Serve over rice.

Helpful Hints: Time spent in the kitchen cooking with your kids is time well spent. You can share the value of preparing wholesome, comforting, nurturing foods while equipping them with the skills to create their own food traditions in the future. Even young children can participate in family meal preparation. Just remember these basics: Always make sure children are well-supervised in the kitchen. Only adults should use sharp utensils, plug in or turn on electric appliances or handle hot foods. Be sure to only assign tasks that the child can do and feel good about.

Makes 6 servings

Gratin Potatoes with Asiago Cheese

Arroz Con Queso

Gratin Potatoes with Asiago Cheese

6	slices bacon, cut into 1-inch pieces
6	medium baking potatoes, peeled and thinly sliced
½	cup grated Asiago cheese
	Salt and black pepper, to taste
1½	cups heavy cream

Cook Time: 7 to 9 hours (LOW) or 5 to 6 hours (HIGH)

1. Heat skillet over medium heat until hot. Add bacon. Cook and stir until crispy. Transfer to paper towel-lined plate with slotted spoon to drain.

2. Pour bacon fat from skillet into 5- to 6-quart **CROCK-POT®** slow cooker. Layer one fourth of potatoes on bottom of **CROCK-POT®** slow cooker. Sprinkle one fourth of bacon over potatoes and top with one fourth of cheese. Add salt and pepper. Repeat layers. Pour cream over all. Cover; cook on LOW 7 to 9 hours or on HIGH 5 to 6 hours. Adjust salt and pepper, if desired.

Makes 4 to 6 servings

Arroz Con Queso

1	can (16 ounces) whole tomatoes, crushed
1	can (15 ounces) black beans, rinsed and drained
1½	cups uncooked long-grain converted rice
1	onion, chopped
1	cup cottage cheese
1	can (4 ounces) chopped green chilies
2	tablespoons vegetable oil
3	teaspoons minced garlic
2	cups grated Monterey Jack cheese, divided

Cook Time: 6 to 9 hours (LOW)

Combine tomatoes, beans, rice, onion, cottage cheese, chilies, oil, garlic and 1 cup cheese in 4½-quart **CROCK-POT®** slow cooker; mix thoroughly. Cover; cook on LOW 6 to 9 hours or until liquid is absorbed. Sprinkle with remaining cheese before serving.

Makes 8 to 10 servings

Boston Baked Beans

Wild Rice with Fruit & Nuts

Boston Baked Beans

2	**pounds small dry white beans**
12	**cups water**
	Olive oil
¼	**cup finely chopped salt pork or thick-sliced bacon**
1	**cup molasses**
½	**cup chopped onions**
½	**cup packed dark brown sugar**
2	**tablespoons dry mustard**
2	**teaspoons salt**

Cook Time: 10 to 12 hours (LOW) or 6 to 8 hours (HIGH)

1. Soak beans in water in uncovered 5-quart **CROCK-POT®** slow cooker overnight (or a minimum of 8 hours). After soaking, cover; cook on LOW 3 hours. Drain liquid, reserving 1 cup. Remove beans; set aside

2. Heat oil in skillet over medium heat until hot. Add salt pork. Cook and stir 5 to 10 minutes to render fat. Remove with slotted spoon and drain on paper towels. Transfer to **CROCK-POT®** slow cooker

3. Add reserved 1 cup cooking liquid, beans, and remaining ingredients, and stir well to combine. Cover; cook on LOW 10 to 12 hours or on HIGH 6 to 8 hours.

Makes 8 servings

Wild Rice with Fruit & Nuts

2	**cups wild rice (or wild rice blend), rinsed***
½	**cup dried cranberries**
½	**cup chopped raisins**
½	**cup chopped dried apricots**
½	**cup almond slivers, toasted****
5	**to 6 cups chicken broth**
1	**cup orange juice**
2	**tablespoons butter, melted**
1	**teaspoon ground cumin**
2	**green onions, thinly sliced**
2	**to 3 tablespoons chopped fresh parsley**
	Salt and black pepper, to taste

Cook Time: 7 hours (LOW) or 2½ to 3 hours (HIGH)

1. Combine wild rice, cranberries, raisins, apricots and almonds in **CROCK-POT®** slow cooker.

2. Combine broth, orange juice, butter and cumin in medium bowl. Pour mixture over rice and stir to mix.

3. Cover; cook on LOW 7 hours or on HIGH 2½ to 3 hours. Stir once, adding more hot broth if necessary.

4. When rice is soft, add green onions and parsley. Adjust seasonings, if desired. Cook 10 minutes longer and serve.

Makes 6 to 8 servings

*Do not use parboiled rice or a blend containing parboiled rice.

**To toast almonds, spread in single layer in heavy-bottomed skillet. Cook over medium heat 1 to 2 minutes, stirring frequently, until nuts are lightly browned. Remove from skillet immediately. Cool before using.

Mediterranean Red Potatoes

Macaroni and Cheese

CROCK·POT
• THE ORIGINAL SLOW COOKER •

Mediterranean Red Potatoes

3 medium red potatoes, cut into bite-size pieces

⅔ cup fresh or frozen pearl onions

Garlic-flavored cooking spray

¾ teaspoon Italian seasoning

¼ teaspoon black pepper

1 small tomato, seeded and chopped

2 ounces (½ cup) crumbled feta cheese

2 tablespoons chopped black olives

Cook Time: 7 to 8 hours (LOW)

1. Place potatoes and onions in 1½-quart soufflé dish. Spray potatoes and onions with cooking spray; toss to coat. Add Italian seasoning and pepper; mix well. Cover dish tightly with foil.

2. Tear off 3 (18×3-inch) strips of heavy-duty foil. Cross strips to resemble wheel spokes. Place soufflé dish in center of strips. Pull foil strips up and over dish to make handles and place dish into **CROCK-POT®** slow cooker.

3. Pour hot water into **CROCK-POT®** slow cooker to about 1½ inches from top of soufflé dish. Cover; cook on LOW 7 to 8 hours.

4. Use foil handles to lift dish out of slow cooker. Stir tomato, feta cheese and olives into potato mixture.

Makes 4 servings

CROCK·POT
• THE ORIGINAL SLOW COOKER •

Macaroni and Cheese

6 cups cooked macaroni

2 tablespoons butter

4 cups evaporated milk

6 cups (24 ounces) shredded Cheddar cheese

2 teaspoons salt

½ teaspoon black pepper

Cook Time: 2 to 3 hours (HIGH)

In large mixing bowl, toss macaroni with butter. Stir in evaporated milk, cheese, salt and pepper; place in 4½-quart **CROCK-POT®** slow cooker. Cover; cook on HIGH 2 to 3 hours.

Makes 6 to 8 servings

Tip: Make this mac 'n' cheese recipe more fun. Add some tasty mix-ins: diced green or red bell pepper, peas, hot dog slices, chopped tomato, browned ground beef, chopped onion. Be creative!

Herbed Fall Vegetables

Creamy Curried Spinach

Herbed Fall Vegetables

2 medium Yukon gold potatoes, peeled and cut into ½-inch dice

2 medium sweet potatoes, peeled and cut into ½-inch dice

3 parsnips, peeled and cut into ½-inch dice

1 medium head of fennel, sliced and cut into ½-inch dice

½ to ¾ cup chopped fresh herbs, such as tarragon, parsley, sage or thyme

4 tablespoons (½ stick) butter, cut into small pieces

1 cup chicken broth

1 tablespoon Dijon mustard

1 tablespoon salt

Freshly ground black pepper to taste

Cook Time: 4½ hours (LOW) or 3 hours (HIGH)

1. Combine potatoes, parsnips, fennel, herbs and butter in 4½-quart **CROCK-POT®** slow cooker.

2. Whisk together broth, mustard, salt and pepper in small bowl. Pour mixture over vegetables. Cover; cook on LOW 4½ hours or on HIGH 3 hours or until vegetables are tender, stirring occasionally to ensure even cooking.

Makes 6 servings

Creamy Curried Spinach

3 packages (10 ounces each) frozen spinach, thawed

1 onion, chopped

4 teaspoons minced garlic

2 tablespoons curry powder

2 tablespoons butter, melted

¼ cup chicken broth

¼ cup heavy cream

1 teaspoon lemon juice

Cook Time: 3 to 4 hours (LOW) or 2 hours (HIGH)

Combine spinach, onion, garlic, curry powder, butter and broth in **CROCK-POT®** slow cooker. Cover; cook on LOW 3 to 4 hours or on HIGH 2 hours or until done. Stir in cream and lemon juice 30 minutes before end of cooking time.

Makes 6 to 8 servings

Cheesy Broccoli Casserole

Orange-Spiced Sweet Potatoes

Cheesy Broccoli Casserole

2 packages (10 ounces each) frozen chopped broccoli, thawed

1 can (10¾ ounces) condensed cream of celery soup, undiluted

1¼ cups shredded sharp Cheddar cheese, divided

¼ cup minced onion

½ teaspoon celery seed

1 teaspoon paprika

1 teaspoon hot pepper sauce

1 cup crushed potato chips or saltine crackers

Cook Time: 5 to 6 hours (LOW) or 2½ to 3 hours (HIGH)

1. Coat 4½-quart **CROCK-POT®** slow cooker with nonstick cooking spray. Combine broccoli, soup, 1 cup cheese, onion, celery seed, paprika and hot sauce in **CROCK-POT®** slow cooker; mix well. Cover; cook on LOW 5 to 6 hours or on HIGH 2½ to 3 hours, or until done.

2. Uncover; sprinkle top with potato chips and remaining ¼ cup cheese. Cook, uncovered, on LOW 30 to 60 minutes or on HIGH 15 to 30 minutes, or until cheese melts.

Makes 4 to 6 servings

Tip: For a change in taste, prepare with thawed chopped spinach instead of broccoli, and top with crushed crackers or spicy croutons to complement the cheesy crust.

Orange-Spiced Sweet Potatoes

2 pounds sweet potatoes, peeled and diced

½ cup packed dark brown sugar

½ cup (1 stick) butter, cut into small pieces

1 teaspoon ground cinnamon

½ teaspoon ground nutmeg

¼ teaspoon grated orange peel

Juice of 1 medium orange

¼ teaspoon salt

1 teaspoon vanilla

Chopped toasted pecans (optional)

Cook Time: 4 hours (LOW) or 2 hours (HIGH)

Place all ingredients, except pecans, in **CROCK-POT®** slow cooker. Cover; cook on LOW 4 hours or on HIGH 2 hours or until potatoes are tender. Sprinkle with pecans before serving, if desired.

Makes 8 servings

Tip: For a creamy variation, mash potatoes with a hand masher or electric mixer, and add ¼ cup milk or whipping cream for moist consistency. Sprinkle with cinnamon-sugar, and sprinkle on toasted pecans, if desired.

CROCK·POT
· THE ORIGINAL SLOW COOKER ·

Gingerbread

Caramel and Apple Pound Cake

Gingerbread

½ cup (1 stick) butter, softened
½ cup sugar
1 egg, lightly beaten
1 cup light molasses
2½ cups all-purpose flour
1½ teaspoons baking soda
1 teaspoon ground cinnamon
2 teaspoons ground ginger
½ teaspoon ground cloves
½ teaspoon salt
1 cup hot water
Whipped cream (optional)

Cook Time: 1½ to 1¾ hours (HIGH)

1. Coat 4½-quart **CROCK-POT®** slow cooker with butter or nonstick cooking spray. Beat together butter and sugar in large bowl. Add egg, molasses, flour, baking soda, cinnamon, ginger, cloves and salt. Stir in hot water and mix well. Pour batter into **CROCK-POT®** slow cooker.

2. Cover; cook on HIGH 1½ to 1¾ hours, or until toothpick inserted into center of cake comes out clean. Serve warm; top with whipped cream, if desired.

Makes 6 to 8 servings

Caramel and Apple Pound Cake

4 medium baking apples, cored, peeled and cut into wedges
½ cup apple juice
½ pound caramels, unwrapped
¼ cup creamy peanut butter
1½ teaspoons vanilla
½ teaspoon ground cinnamon
⅛ teaspoon ground cardamon
1 prepared pound cake, sliced

Cook Time: 7 to 9 hours (LOW) or 4 to 5 hours (HIGH)

1. Coat inside of **CROCK-POT®** slow cooker with nonstick cooking spray. Layer apples, apple juice and caramels in **CROCK-POT®** slow cooker.

2. Mix together peanut butter, vanilla, cinnamon and cardamom in small bowl. Drop by teaspoons onto apples. Cover; cook on LOW 6 to 8 hours or on HIGH 3 to 4 hours.

3. Stir thoroughly, and cook 1 hour longer. To serve, spoon warm over cake slices.

Makes 6 to 8 servings

Fudge and Cream Pudding Cake

Cinnamon-Ginger Poached Pears

Fudge and Cream Pudding Cake

2 tablespoons unsalted butter

1 cup all-purpose flour

¾ cup packed light brown sugar

5 tablespoons unsweetened cocoa powder, divided

2 teaspoons baking powder

½ teaspoon ground cinnamon

⅛ teaspoon salt

1 cup light cream

1 tablespoon vegetable oil

1 teaspoon vanilla

¾ cup packed dark brown sugar

1¾ cups hot water

Whipped cream or ice cream (optional)

Cook Time: 2 hours (HIGH)

1. Coat inside of 4½-quart **CROCK-POT®** slow cooker with butter. Combine flour, light brown sugar, 3 tablespoons cocoa, baking powder, cinnamon and salt in medium bowl. Add cream, oil and vanilla; stir well to combine. Pour batter into **CROCK-POT®** slow cooker.

2. Combine dark brown sugar and remaining 2 tablespoons cocoa in medium bowl. Add hot water; stir well to combine. Pour sauce over cake batter. Do not stir. Cover; cook on HIGH 2 hours.

3. Spoon portions of pudding cake onto plate. Serve with whipped cream, if desired.

Makes 8 to 10 servings

Cinnamon-Ginger Poached Pears

3 cups water

1 cup sugar

10 slices fresh ginger

2 whole cinnamon sticks

1 tablespoon chopped candied ginger (optional)

6 Bosc or Anjou pears, peeled and cored

Cook Time: 4½ to 6½ hours (LOW) or 2 to 2½ hours (HIGH)

1. Combine water, sugar, ginger, cinnamon and candied ginger, if desired, in 4½-quart **CROCK-POT®** slow cooker. Add pears. Cover; cook on LOW 4 to 6 hours or on HIGH 1½ to 2 hours.

2. Remove pears. Cook syrup, uncovered, 30 minutes or until thickened.

Makes 6 servings

Pineapple Rice Pudding

Classic Baked Apples

Pineapple Rice Pudding

1 can (20 ounces) crushed pineapple in juice, undrained

1 can (13½ ounces) coconut milk

1 can (12 ounces) fat-free evaporated milk

¾ cup uncooked arborio rice

2 eggs, lightly beaten

¼ cup granulated sugar

¼ cup packed light brown sugar

½ teaspoon ground cinnamon

¼ teaspoon ground nutmeg

¼ teaspoon salt

Toasted coconut* and pineapple slices (optional)

*To toast coconut, spread evenly on ungreased baking sheet. Toast in preheated 350°F oven 5 to 7 minutes, stirring occasionally, until light golden brown.

Cook Time: 3 to 4 hours (HIGH)

1. Place pineapple with juice, coconut milk, evaporated milk, rice, eggs, sugar, brown sugar, cinnamon, nutmeg and salt into **CROCK-POT®** slow cooker; mix well. Cover; cook on high 3 to 4 hours or until thickened and rice is tender.

2. Stir until blended. Serve warm or chilled. Garnish with toasted coconut and pineapple, if desired.

Makes 8 servings

Classic Baked Apples

¼ cup packed dark brown sugar

2 tablespoons golden raisins

1 teaspoon grated lemon peel

6 small to medium baking apples, washed and cored

1 teaspoon ground cinnamon

2 tablespoons butter, cut into small pieces

¼ cup orange juice

¼ cup water

Whipped cream (optional)

Cook Time: 7 to 9 hours (LOW) or 2½ to 3½ hours (HIGH)

1. Combine brown sugar, raisins and lemon peel in small bowl. Fill core of each apple with mixture. Place apples in 4½-quart **CROCK-POT®** slow cooker. Sprinkle with cinnamon and dot with butter. Pour orange juice and water over apples. Cover; cook on LOW 7 to 9 hours or on HIGH 2½ to 3½ hours.

2. To serve, place apples in individual bowls. Top with sauce. Garnish with whipped cream, if desired.

Makes 4 serving

Triple Delicious Hot Chocolate

Mulled Apple Cider

Triple Delicious Hot Chocolate

⅓ cup sugar

¼ cup unsweetened cocoa powder

¼ teaspoon salt

3 cups milk, divided

¾ teaspoon vanilla

1 cup heavy cream

1 square (1 ounce) bittersweet chocolate

1 square (1 ounce) white chocolate

¾ cup whipped cream

6 teaspoons mini chocolate chips or shaved bittersweet chocolate

Cook Time: 2 hours (LOW)

1. Combine sugar, cocoa, salt and ½ cup milk in medium bowl. Beat until smooth. Transfer to 4½-quart **CROCK-POT®** slow cooker. Add remaining 2½ cups milk and vanilla; stir in. Cover; cook on LOW 2 hours.

2. Add cream. Cover; cook on LOW 10 minutes. Stir in bittersweet and white chocolates until melted.

3. Pour hot chocolate into 6 coffee cups. Top each serving with 2 tablespoons whipped cream and 1 teaspoon chocolate chips.

Makes 6 servings

Mulled Apple Cider

2 quarts bottled apple cider or juice (not unfiltered)

¼ cup packed light brown sugar

1 square (8 inches) double-thickness cheesecloth

8 allspice berries

4 cinnamon sticks, broken into halves

12 whole cloves

1 large orange

Additional cinnamon sticks (optional)

Cook Time: 2½ to 3 hours (HIGH)

1. Combine apple cider and brown sugar in 4½-quart **CROCK-POT®** slow cooker.

2. Rinse cheesecloth; squeeze out water. Wrap allspice berries and cinnamon stick halves in cheesecloth; tie securely with cotton string or strip of cheesecloth.

3. Stick cloves randomly into orange; cut orange into quarters. Place spice bag and orange quarters in cider mixture. Cover; cook on HIGH 2½ to 3 hours.

4. Once cooked, **CROCK-POT®** slow cooker may be turned to LOW to keep cider warm up to 3 additional hours. Remove and discard spice bag and orange before serving. Ladle cider into mugs. Garnish with additional cinnamon sticks, if desired.

Makes 10 servings

Tip: To make inserting cloves into the orange a little easier, first pierce the orange skin with the point of wooden skewer. Remove the skewer and insert a clove.